"Tri Robinson helps me understand how God's land, our life development, and the Lord's ministry can be integrated. Like Jesus, he tells us stories that change our lives. I loved reading this book!"

Dr. Joel C. Hunter, senior pastor of Northland,
A Church Distributed, Longwood, FL

"Tri Robinson's vivid prose and rich metaphors make discipleship come alive. In story after story he reveals the power and beauty of God's love and desire to personally engage us. I want to become the 'spiritual horticulturalist' that *Rooted in Good Soil* describes. Tri's vulnerability and experiences inspire me to more deeply surrender to Jesus. This is the real deal."

Dave Workman, pastor and author of
The Outward-Focused Life

"I have liked and admired Tri Robinson for twenty years. In *Rooted in Good Soil*, he brings together the keen, curious, and sharp mind of a teacher; the wise experience of a farmer; the warm heart of a disciple; and the expert guidance of a veteran pastor. If you're interested in how followership of Jesus really works, read this simple, enjoyable book."

Todd Hunter, founder of Churches for the Sake of Others;
pastor of Holy Trinity Church, Costa Mesa, CA

"*Rooted in Good Soil* is a wonderfully warm and insightful book that gleans lessons on the Christian life from the rich soil of farming experiences in the Idaho Cascades. Tri Robinson is perfectly suited to the subject. He has an undergraduate degree in biology and has farmed the land for many years. He also has planted and pastored a thriving church, excelled in leadership, and discipled many new believers. This combination of horticultural knowledge and leadership experience has resulted in a delightful book for both the beginning traveler on the Christian way and the pilgrim who is a long way down the road."

Berten A. Waggoner, national director, Vineyard USA

"In *Rooted in Good Soil*, Tri Robinson, who has been in full-time ministry for thirty years, shows us how we as Christians can become fruitful disciples of God's Great Commission to bring in a huge harvest for a true relationship with the Lord Jesus. I encourage you to read this deep and inspiring yet easy-to-read book. It is a welcome addition to creation care and missions literature."

Don Richards, director of Suba Environmental Education of Kenya; chairman of Kenya Islands Missions, Inc.

Rooted in Good Soil

Cultivating and Sustaining
Authentic Discipleship

Tri Robinson

BakerBooks

a division of Baker Publishing Group
Grand Rapids, Michigan

Published by Baker Books
a division of Baker Publishing Group
P.O. Box 6287, Grand Rapids, MI 49516-6287
www.bakerbooks.com

Printed in the United States of America

Library of Congress Cataloging-in-Publication Data
Robinson, Tri, 1948–
    Rooted in good soil : cultivating and sustaining authentic discipleship / Tri Robinson.
        p. cm. — (Shapevine)
    ISBN 978-0-8010-7253-6 (pbk.)
    1. Christian life. 2. Sower (Parable) 3. Robinson, Tri, 1948– 4. Farm life—Religious aspects—Christianity. I. Title.
    BV4501.3.R643 2010
    248.4—dc22   2009049427

Unless otherwise noted, Scripture quotations are taken from the HOLY BIBLE, NEW INTERNATIONAL VERSION®. NIV®. Copyright © 1973, 1978, 1984 by International Bible Society. Used by permission of Zondervan. All rights reserved.

Scripture marked AMP is taken from the Amplified® Bible, Copyright © 1954, 1958, 1962, 1964, 1965, 1987 by The Lockman Foundation. Used by permission.

Scripture marked NASB is taken from the New American Standard Bible®, Copyright © 1960, 1962, 1963, 1968, 1971, 1972, 1973, 1975, 1977, 1995 by The Lockman Foundation. Used by permission.

Scripture marked NLT is taken from the *Holy Bible*, New Living Translation, copyright © 1996, 2004. Used by permission of Tyndale House Publishers, Inc., Wheaton, Illinois 60189. All rights reserved.

10   11   12   13   14   15   16   7   6   5   4   3   2   1

My personal life has become "rooted in God's good soil" because of the prayers, love, and dedication of my wife, Nancy. She is my gift from God, and the reason I have a story to tell.

Contents

About the Shapevine Missional Series

The key purpose of Shapevine the organization is to bring the various elements of missional Christianity—namely, church planting movements, urban mission, the emerging church, the missional church movement, the organic/simple church, and marketplace ministries—into meaningful dialogue around the truly big ideas of our time. Consistent with this purpose, the Shapevine Missional Series in partnership with Baker Books seeks to bring innovative thinking to the missional issues of church planting, mission, evangelism, social justice, and anything in between.

We seek to publish both established authors as well as others who have significant things to contribute but have operated largely under the radar.

The series will focus on three distinctive areas:

- **Living—Practical Missional Orthopraxy**
  Orthopraxy is what makes orthodoxy worth having. We yearn for the experience and continual

flow of living out the gospel message in our day-to-day lives for the sake of others. The stories and ideas in the Shapevine Missional Series are aimed at providing practical handles and means to wrap our readers' minds around the idea of living as the people of God, sent into the world with the Spirit and impulse of Jesus himself.

- **Learning—Solid Missional Orthodoxy**
  Jesus both lived and proclaimed a theology of a missional God. His was and is a message of mercy, justice, and goodness toward others. It was this message that erupted into the greatest movement in the history of humankind. The same God who sent his only Son now sends those who follow his Son, in the same manner and with the same message. This is at the heart of a missional theology.

- **Leading—Tools for Missional Leadership**
  Our aim is for the books in this series to serve as tools for pastors, organizational leaders, and church members throughout the world to equip themselves and others as they travel the path of faithfulness in the missional life.

As a global interactive forum, Shapevine allows anyone to both learn and contribute at whatever level suits. To learn more, go to www.shapevine.com or contact us at info@shapevine.com.

Alan Hirsch and Lance Ford

Series Editor's Preface

To say that issues relating to the environment affect us all is surely an understatement; as far as we know, this is the only planet we can live on. Muck around with the environment and we change the very life conditions of billions of people, including the reader of this book. The scenario of a disaster of global proportions is now not just a piece of intriguing science fiction; it is a very real possibility, if not an inevitability. And because the environment affects us all, it surely should concern us all.

The God of creation is the God of redemption; therefore, what is true for ecology in general is true for the spiritual life in particular. There is something *ecological* about the life of prayer, discipleship, and mission. Taking his cues from soils, plants, life, and nature, Tri Robinson helps us see the life of the Spirit/spirit more clearly.

This book is part of the Shapevine-Baker line because we strongly believe worship, discipleship, spirituality, and mission are all connected in God's ecology, and that true holiness is not some otherworldly enterprise but rather is something intrinsically concerned with redeeming people, loving place, and humanely caring for the plight of animals and the earth.

Taking the incarnation of God in Jesus as our missional cue, we find ourselves located in this place, in this distinct time, and among this particular people. We take this seriously because we are called not just to eternal salvation as "pie in the sky when you die," but to witness here and now to what it means to live out in real-time situations and circumstances the holy and wholesome life of God.

Tri Robinson proves to be a wonderful guide in spiritual matters. His unique brand of eco-spirituality shows us how to love God in creation as we ought and also helps us locate mission and discipleship as part of a life of prayer and worship. Not only does he believe this stuff as some sort of ideology and as an active leader of a busy Vineyard church in Boise, but he and the community live it out in tangible and world-redeeming ways.

Biblical spirituality has always looked to creation for metaphors for what life in God should look like. In some ways, this book is not new. Rather, it is a renovation of an oft-forgotten dimension of spiritual life.

Alan Hirsch, series editor

Introduction

I wasn't expecting it, I didn't ask for it, and I definitely didn't see it coming.

I had just begun full-time ministry in the early 1980s when I had the wonderful privilege of spending time with Bobby Clinton, head of the leadership department at Fuller Seminary. He shared a concept with me that he called *convergence*. He said *convergence* was one of the last phases of leadership; it occurs when a leader's gift mix, experience, and temperament all merge together, causing leadership to flow naturally.

This idea had little impact on me in those early days of ministry. More than twenty-five years later, however, it has come to full reality. What I did not understand as a new leader is now, after a lifetime of experience, bringing about true convergence, manifested in a more natural and organic style of leadership. Simply put, I am now able to lead with greater confidence, trusting in whom God has created me to be. It has been like being born again—again.

As I look back now, I can identify some defining moments not only in my ministry but also in my life. Throughout those years a myriad of thoughts, desires, life experiences (good and bad), disillusionments, dreams, and expectations collided like a great train wreck.

Actually they had been on a collision course for years, but early one morning in the late 1990s, they were destined to converge. It happened as I sat in my overstuffed chair preparing for another Sunday message. But this train wreck did not end in disaster and crisis; instead it produced a great blast of light that illuminated a whole new course of action. It changed how I would pursue ministry and life from that point on.

Retrospect is wonderful. Ten years later, I am amazed at how clearly I can visualize the collision. Although many trains were on this collision course, I will share four that I see as the most relevant.

A Collision Course

I had been a pastor for nearly twenty years, ten of those in a church my wife, Nancy, and I planted with a great team in Boise, Idaho. This was during the "church growth movement." In those days every pastor knew success would ultimately be defined by numbers, by how many warm bodies were present on any given Sunday morning. Ultimate success became known as the "mega church." The growth of the assembly was esteemed far more than any individual's personal spiritual growth. Buying into the belief that success was defined more by quantity of people than by quality of discipleship was that first train heading for collision.

The second train was more personal. It concerned a close friend of mine I will call Tom. I had been Tom's pastor for years. I attended his wedding, dedicated his babies, and enjoyed his friendship outside of the church, doing various projects and going on camping trips together. He was a gentle, outgoing guy you couldn't help but like. Tom almost never missed church and was diligent to raise his family in Christian fellowship.

I thought I knew Tom pretty well—until the day he began to drink. Within six months he was drinking a fifth of vodka a day; and in a matter of two years he had completely blown his life apart, losing his family and his job.

Tom's story is an extreme one, but he represented many whose lives in Christ never seemed to go beyond a surface relationship. It became apparent to me that many people did not have their spiritual roots established in the depth of God's mercy and grace. As a result, they soon drifted away looking for comfort, an emotional fix outside of Christ. What bothered me most was how ineffective I felt I had been as Tom's pastor and his Christian friend. Tom and others like him were riding in my second train.

The third train was related to a conversation many of my contemporaries were having at the time. It was a conversation that made many of us insecure regarding our ministry methodology. During the late nineties, it seemed as though every new book and leadership gathering wrestled with the transition from modernity to postmodernity. It forced us to question ourselves as leaders. We wanted desperately to be effective in this new emerging culture and generation but did not have a clue what to do about it. Nothing at this time was tested but everything was tried. Only the successful mega churches could afford the new technology and level of excellence that were being touted, while others tried to reinvent and redefine church in ways that seemed at times nonbiblical. I was filled with confusion; this confusion and questioning stirred up the insecurity that rode in my third train.

On the fourth train was not crisis or despair but many cars linked together that carried my personal desires and dreams apart from ministry or church. I have a deep love for the land and would even describe myself as an environmentalist. In the nineties I was afraid to admit this in Christian circles, fearing I would be misunderstood and marginalized. Years later I wrote the book *Saving God's Green Earth*, which called Christians to the responsibility of creation care. But in those early days, this sort of thing was completely unheard of, even though for years Nancy and I had been trying to live an ecologically sustainable lifestyle.

For the first twenty years of our marriage, we lived on a small homestead that had been in my family for five generations. We raised our two children on that peaceful ranch, many of those years without electricity. We grew much of our own food. In addition to our earthy lifestyle, I taught biology and science at the secondary level for twelve years before entering full-time ministry. Mixing Christianity and science was also somewhat taboo, and so I found myself living two separate lives. This made up the fourth train headed for collision.

Convergence

Undoubtedly many other trains divinely converged that morning as I sat in my study with my Bible on my lap.

I was silently contemplating the passage I would be unpacking before the church on the following Sunday. I don't remember the exact Gospel I was in, but the Scripture told the familiar parable Jesus taught about the sower and the four soils. This story appears in all three synoptic Gospels, which perhaps underscores its importance to God and to us.

It's a familiar story, one I had read many times; but in that moment of convergence, it jumped off the page into my life. As all those trains of thoughts and emotions collided, the desire to grow a big church simply for growth's sake left me. The hunger to minister deeply to people like Tom surged within, and the ways and means to do it were revealed. The desire to build a relevant, culture-changing church where Christians translated grace and mercy into real life seemed doable.

Finally my understanding and appreciation for a natural, organic, and sustainable life were not to be segregated from ministry but integrated into the very process. After all, none other than Jesus told of a farmer who went out to sow seed, and the seed could not take root in soil that was hard and rocky or filled with choking thistles. In three of the four scenarios presented in the parable, the seed did not last. It was picked away, it didn't take root due to the quality of soil, or it was choked out by cares of the world. In the good soil, however, it bore fruit and produced a great outward harvest. In the good soil, the seed was able to establish roots that grew deep and strong into the love of God, resulting in an authentic, lasting maturity. Although Jesus does not tell us what the good soil represents, I believe it is the reality of God's love as it connects with the reality of life—the pain, struggles, and experiences that impact human development.

The answer to everything I had dreamed of was hidden in the good soil. This epiphany would forever challenge me to take Jesus and his parable at its word and look hard into the mystery of the good soil. If it was in the good soil that true Christianity took root, it was incumbent on me to understand how this truth could be translated into changed human life. I wanted to put this knowledge to work in a church that could consistently produce mature, authentic, fruitful, and outreaching Christian people.

1

Finding the Secret of the Harvest

The Condition of the Soil

Sometimes it is difficult to communicate an emotional experience and all it entails because often the people experiencing it do not fully comprehend it themselves. One such experience happened to me on a beautiful June morning, totally catching me by surprise.

I had been baling hay for a few hours on a ten-acre field of our newly established eighty-acre farmstead in Idaho. I had been working since early morning pulling my recently acquired, old New Holland baler behind an equally dated International tractor. The sun had just risen, and in the early light I looked back across the field with great satisfaction, seeing perfectly strung bundles of hay lying neatly in my wake. It was the firstfruits of a harvest I had been dreaming about for years. I had never considered myself a farmer. I had never run a baler, and to be perfectly candid, I did not know how a machine of its vintage could bundle, compress, and tie knots around a pile of loose hay. To me, it was nothing short of a miracle to watch those bales drop to the field.

As I sat there and reminisced about the many years Nancy and I had dreamed, planned, saved, and sacrificed to make this moment a reality, I was lost in wonder. While pondering this, I saw our old brown ranch truck and flatbed trailer ambling toward me from the adjacent field. It pulled up beside me and Nancy jumped out, escorted by our two enthusiastic yellow Labs, Jenny and Lily.

> *The harvest I was physically experiencing in my hay field symbolized a greater harvest in our personal lives.*

It was more than my heart could bear. I was so overwhelmed with gratitude and thanksgiving, I broke into tears, which seemed inappropriate as I sat up there on that man-sized diesel tractor.

Those tears came with the realization that God had fulfilled a vision and lifelong desire that Nancy and I had during nearly forty years of marriage. In that moment it hit me head-on how good the Lord is and how faithful he had been to us. The harvest I was physically experiencing in my hay field symbolized a greater harvest in our personal lives, a harvest produced through tenacity—years of hard work and the determination to trust God for his provision.

Humble Beginnings

Even before our marriage in 1970, Nancy and I spent hours together sharing our hopes and dreams as many young couples do. We had a common love of the land and anticipated the adventure of breaking the status quo of American normality. We dreamed of homesteading and living not *off* the land but *with* it. We didn't know the terminology to describe it then, but today we would use words such as "organic" and "sustainable." We envisioned a vegetable garden, farm animals, and even the use of horse power to work the land. It was a big vision, and it wasn't going to come easily.

After I completed my master's degree at the College of Idaho in Caldwell, we moved onto a small ranch homestead that had been in my family for four generations. Amazingly, those dreams of harvesting off the land were becoming a reality. Or so we thought.

Nancy and I drove our 1965 VW bug more than eight hundred miles across mountains and deserts to the front gate of Robinson Canyon Ranch in Southern California. We packed our VW with all we owned, plus our newly acquired Labrador puppy, Blue. We arrived in mid-February only to discover that the quarter-mile drive up the mountain was covered with three feet of fresh snow. So in trip after trip, we packed our few possessions on our backs and hiked up the hillside to the rather primitive cabin that we would call home for the next twenty years.

Robinson Canyon Ranch was located an hour from the nearest town. Due to the remoteness of the ranch, it was without electricity or phone service. Water was supplied by a mountain-fed spring, which my great-grandfather had piped in from a mile up the canyon years before.

That first winter was a real adventure for a newlywed couple, especially considering that Nancy was raised in San Diego and, with the exception of two short years in Idaho, had never been out of the big city. It was a long and cold winter in a cabin that had no insulation in the walls and leaky windows that let in the bitter cold. The kitchen, dining area, and living room made up one common room. In the kitchen stood my great-grandmother's original woodstove, and in the living room was a large rock fireplace that my father built when I was three years old. Years later I can still recall playing in the sand as a small child while my dad mixed it with cement to make mortar for the fireplace.

The cabin was crude, cold, and remote, but it possessed everything we had dreamed of in those earlier idealistic conversations as a young couple making plans for the future. We closed off the bedrooms and lived for the first three or four months in the common room, keeping the fireplace fed day and night with massive oak logs. Nancy and I still laugh as we recollect hearing Blue yelping in the wee hours of the morning after crawling into the ashes of the fireplace looking for warmth but finding a very hot coal instead.

It definitely wasn't a first year of marriage I would recommend to most couples, but one thing was certain—we got to know each other very well in those early days. We rarely left the ranch, only venturing out about once a month to visit family or pick up supplies from town. At that time we were living on two hundred dollars a month, which our family gave us so we could work on the early development of the ranch.

The cabin sat on a small bench on the south slope of Liebre Mountain in a grove of gigantic Digger Pines and grand oak trees. During the winter months, the sunshine had a hard time finding our small home, and the snow usually stayed until the last weeks of March. Spring was a welcome sight and as soon as the ground appeared, we began to clear acres of mountain mahogany and sagebrush from around the cabin. We needed bare ground not just for our small horticulture projects but for fire safety and the removal of a prolific rattlesnake habitat. That first summer we killed nine large timber rattlesnakes right around the cabin, some of which measured more than four feet in length. Several years earlier my younger sister had been bitten by two of these large snakes at the same time and had nearly died. We developed a healthy respect for them, and Nancy soon became proficient with my old double-barrel twelve-gauge shotgun.

With my dad's help, we planted an orchard with a variety of fruit trees, cultivated the virgin but rocky mountain-side soil in preparation for our vegetable garden, and built fences to hold our first livestock. The cabin was fitted with propane gaslights, which we supplemented with Coleman lanterns. We kept our food cold in an old propane Serville refrigerator. Because the cabin lacked storage and cabinets, we needed a place to store food at a constant temperature, especially Nancy's canned goods. We decided to dig and construct a root cellar in the hillside behind the kitchen. In those days, everything we did we had to do by hand. For weeks I worked with pick and shovel and a long steel bar, prying loose huge granite boulders. Every morning I would get up early, before the day became too hot, and tell Nancy I was going out to work on the hole. From that time on, the root cellar that served our young family for many years became fondly known as "the Hole."

A mile down the road was a neighboring ranch that once belonged to my grandfather. Then the Griffin family, who lived two hours away in Hollywood, owned it. Although the Griffins came up on the weekends, during the week it was operated by an older couple who served as their foremen for many years.

The things we were learning were far more than lessons in agriculture; they were deep truths about developing and nurturing ourselves and others into mature and sustainable Christian people.

Larry and Clara Pilgrim were the salt of the earth. They had spent years living the life Nancy and I dreamed of and became a wealth of information to us. In many ways they were our first mentors in sustainable living. They taught us how to plant vegetables and what would grow best in the soil and climate of the mountain. They supplied us with such valuable commodities as cow manure and used fencing wire. Clara mentored Nancy in skills like canning and preserving food that was proudly stored in "the Hole." In trade Nancy helped Clara pluck and clean chickens, quite a stretch for a girl who had been raised in the city.

Nancy enrolled in a forestry class and learned how to seed and grow various types of pine trees. With the financial backing of my parents, we developed a nursery of our own. We started pine nuts in a seedbed and transferred a thousand tiny seedlings into fifteen-gallon metal containers. We were on a fast learning curve that exposed us to the value of good soil and all that must happen for a tiny fragile seed to take root and grow into a healthy mature rooted plant. We didn't realize it then, but the things we were learning would become some of the most valuable lessons in our later life of ministry. They were far more than lessons in agriculture; they were deep truths about developing and nurturing ourselves and others into mature and sustainable Christian people.

Ranch life taught us much in those early days, especially how to maintain a lasting marriage and the deep joy of raising a family. We learned how to meet the challenge of building natural, sustainable lives, not only physically but also spiritually. We discovered what it meant to have an authentic relationship with Jesus. Although both Nancy and I had been baptized as children, we chose to be baptized together in a swimming pond that took me the better part of a summer to create. The ranch gave us both a deep, lifelong love and appreciation for solitude. In the shadow of the mountain, our love for God was nurtured and an awareness of the richness and purpose of life became magnified. There God gave us a united vision and desire to serve him.

The Importance of Good Soil

As rich as our time on the ranch was, there was one very tough problem: the ranch had very little tillable soil. The ground was too steep, too rocky, and too dry—making it extremely difficult to produce a crop of any substance. It became increasingly apparent that, if we were to live sustainably, we would need land that could support an annual harvest of hay. In some areas there were rich deposits of topsoil, but they were generally surrounded by thick mountain mahogany and other dominating brush. Just beneath the surface were granite rocks of every size and, because the climate was dry, grass hay could grow only in the wet months of spring. By early summer everything dried out to the point of becoming a fire hazard.

Soil conditions are everything if you want to grow a good crop. The same is true in life. Soil conditions are everything if you desire to live a fruitful life. Jesus made this point in the story he told his followers about a sower who went out on the land to plant seed (Matt. 13:1–23). Jesus explained that the sower was God, and the seed was his word (the truth of who he is and his eternal plan for all humanity). He told the story of the seed and how it fell on four different types of ground. Only when the seed fell on good soil did it produce a harvest. In the depths of good soil, the seed could take root and be sustained to the point of growing to maturity and fruitfulness.

In his first three attempts, the sower failed to harvest a mature crop. The seed fell on a hard path, on rocky soil, and on ground filled with choking thorny undergrowth. In all three cases the seed never became substantially rooted. On the hard ground, the first seed couldn't penetrate and was vulnerable to the birds. The hard ground represents a hard heart, where the good seed of God's Word is quickly picked away by the devil and his lies. In this case the seed never had a chance to become established and grow.

In the second scenario, the seed fell on rocky ground. Jesus said this is representative of those who receive the word with joy when they first hear but it doesn't become rooted in their heart. Without deep roots, people believe for only a short while and eventually fall away. This seed grew quickly, developing shallow roots that were unable to maintain and sustain a life of maturity. The Gospel of Matthew attributes this short-lived faith to the injection of life's problems, while

Luke points to "the time of testing" (8:13) or "times of temptation" (NASB) when faith is lost. When real life happens and troubles or temptations come (as they surely will), those whose roots are not deeply established in an authentic relationship with Christ won't be able to make the connection between the truth and life when it counts the most.

The third seed fell on the thorny soil, which represents those whose lives start to take root and begin to grow, but Luke records: "All too quickly the message is crowded out by the cares and riches and pleasures of this life. And so they never grow into maturity" (v. 14 NLT).

Four different scenarios are portrayed in the parable, and of the four, only the seed that fell on good soil grew to spiritual maturity. This is something to note—only one group managed to grow roots that penetrated deep into the love, grace, and mercy of God. Only one group became sustainable to the point of bearing a harvest that could reproduce itself in the lives of others. Looking back on nearly thirty years of full-time ministry, I have seen this simple story played out time and again. How discouraging it has been to see so many people whose life with God started out with great zeal but didn't last. There have been so many who never became fully rooted in truth and have been picked off by the lies of the enemy, the cares and troubles of life, or the lure of worldliness. Often even those I would consider to be Christians miss the richness that can be found only in the depth of the good soil.

Waiting on the Harvest

If you're a Christian leader who has experienced the discouragement of seeing those you've cared for, invested in, and truly loved fall away from faith, I encourage you to join me in a quest. We must discover the mystery of the good soil Jesus spoke of in the parable. If authentic and mature Christianity is to be achieved in the lives of our people, we must rethink discipleship and reevaluate our definition of success. Success can no longer be about the number of people sitting in seats on any given Sunday but rather about what is happening in the lives represented. Are people getting their root base fully established in the depth of God's love so that their lives are producing lasting fruit and a reproducible harvest? Or will their experience with Christ be superficial and short-lived when the storms of life hit? We must become spiritual horticulturalists who fully understand the makeup of good soil so our crops will more consistently grow to maturity, authenticity, and sustainability.

This is my challenge to Christians and Christian leaders alike who have a heart to consistently nurture human life to the fullness of God's intention and divine plan. Only in this way will we ever experience in our lifetime the revival and ultimate cultural reformation we long for and pray to see.

The tears I fought back on my tractor that morning in June were prompted by the reality that God had brought Nancy's and my life full circle. He had fulfilled a lifelong vision to place us on land that encompassed acres of tillable soil. Somehow in that moment of thanksgiving came the realization of the divine connection between the physical harvest I was experiencing and the spiritual harvest for which I longed. Jesus's parable was more than a story; it was the means to a fulfilled life. He was connecting my two worlds—the world of sustainable farming and the world of functional ministry.

It had taken us nearly forty years of dreaming, preparing, and tenacious hard work to experience those first bales of harvested hay. The point was clear: a spiritual harvest of mature and sustainable Christians would also require nothing less than dreaming, preparing, and tenacious hard work, but in the end God's faithfulness and promise would prevail.

Now I realize just how essential good soil is for the harvest. To find the secret of the harvest, I must put all my energies to bear on discovering the mystery of the good soil.

2

Cultivated and Broken

Repentance

One day in late March, Nancy brought me a calendar she had prepared that would provide us with a schedule for planting the vegetable garden through the spring months. She had researched our climatic zone and the recommended planting dates for the varieties of vegetables we had decided to grow that season. It is important to note some vegetables need to be planted earlier in the year than others so they will have a chance to take root and mature before the days lengthen and the air and soil temperatures rise. Peas come first, shortly followed by lettuce, spinach, cabbage, and various root crops like potatoes, onions, and radishes. Looking at her calendar I realized I had better get started right away if we were going to stay on schedule.

Our garden plot lay fallow all winter, and the ground had become hard and compacted after months of being under several feet of snow. I admit I wasn't excited about the work it was going to take to turn over a garden plot the size of ours, especially since it still felt like winter outside. In years past I never started the garden until that warm finger of spring beckoned me outside and the comfortable temperatures encouraged me to stay there. This particular day in March wasn't at all like that. It was windy and cold, and the sky threatened rain or snow. The day was much better suited to doing something indoors. But knowing how important timing can be, I put on my coat reluctantly, grabbed a shovel, and prepared the ground for the first seeds of spring.

Timing and soil preparation are important parts of the process of growing things to maturity, both in plants and in our lives.

The Need for Brokenness

Jesus's parable tells us it was in the good soil where the seed took root, matured, and produced a harvest. Having grown dozens of vegetable gardens in my life, I have learned a few things along the way. First, seasonal timing is crucial; second, making the initial effort to prepare the ground will determine the outcome of the plant. Timing and soil preparation are important parts of the process of growing things to maturity, both in plants and in our lives.

The soils in Jesus's parable of the sower represent your heart and my heart. God wants every one of us to receive his seed and mature spiritually so we will bear fruit. The seed he plants is the truth about who he is, his nature, and his eternal intention for us. He desires to plant the reality of eternity in every person's heart so we might discover not only who he is but who we are in him. His intention is that we capture his good, pleasing, and perfect will, which is the very thing that allows our lives to produce a harvest. In Ecclesiastes 3, King Solomon wrote, "For everything there is a season, a time for every activity under heaven. A time to be born and a time to die. A time to plant and a time to harvest" (vv. 1–2 NLT). Then a few verses later he wrote, "Yet God has made everything beautiful for its own time. He has planted eternity in the human heart, but even so, people cannot see the whole scope of God's work from beginning to end" (v. 11 NLT).

Life has a way of compacting and hardening the soil of our hearts. Life's hurts combined with the gradual accumulation of guilt and shame as a result of sin constantly weigh us down, causing our hearts to become like the soil in my garden after a long and harsh winter.

There are two kinds of sin: the sin we do and the sin others do to us. Either way it is all sin and it is all damaging. The sin we do can produce deep feelings of guilt and shame. The sin others do to us can produce feelings of bitterness, anger, and even rage. Over the course of time, all of this can produce a hardened heart; and like soil, it eventually becomes so crusted over, it is impossible for the seeds of truth to penetrate. Like the soil, until the heart is cultivated and broken, God's truth cannot take root. Therefore brokenness is the first essential event that must occur before the process of spiritual maturity can begin.

Breaking Hard Ground

No one is exempt from the hurts and pain of life. All of us have had things done to us that have caused us to close up and shut others out. All of us have done things to others that we shouldn't have done, and because of our behavior, we have shut God out. The Bible calls it our fallen or sinful nature. In Romans 3:23 Paul said, "For everyone has sinned; we all fall short of God's glorious standard" (NLT). Paul went on to say that through the work of Jesus, God made provision for us to have our past washed clean so that we can have a fresh start and a new beginning. This is the reason the gospel is called the *Good News*—because it really is good news for a hurting world. The good news is that there is a way to break up the fallow ground of our hearts and enter into a life with God that will allow us to produce a great harvest.

The good news is that there is a way to break up the fallow ground of our heart and enter into a life with God that will allow us to produce a great harvest.

When Nancy and I married in 1970, we were two young people intoxicated with love. Our year of courtship and engagement was one of the best times of our lives. She was eighteen, and I was twenty-two, and during that year we spent endless hours together doing all kinds of fun and crazy things. We talked on and on about our lives, our ideals, and our dreams. We shared our pasts, but for some reason at that time in our lives, we never really shared our pain. I'm not sure why that was except that Solomon was right when he said God has a time and season for everything.

To be honest, I think God wanted us to relish the moment and simply enjoy being in love. The honeymoon lasted for about the next two years, and then God began to lift the veil of grace.

Both Nancy and I had been raised in church. She came from a very strong Irish Catholic background, and I came from a long line of Protestants. But it wasn't religion that got in the way of our relationship; it was the absence of God. Although we had been raised in church, neither of us really understood what a relationship with Christ meant.

During those early years, I started my teaching profession in the city that was an hour away from the old ranch. I left in the early morning, taught school all day, and then hurried home in the late afternoon to catch up on all kinds of ranch projects. Nancy, on the other hand, stayed day after day in the isolation of the ranch. It was during those early years of starting a family that Nancy spent many hours alone as a young mother. We had no telephone or electricity on the ranch in those days, so Nancy had very little contact with the outside world. The truth is she had nowhere to turn in her loneliness and pain but to God.

Sometimes I think God lets us try to figure out our lives for a while, waiting for us to realize how much we really need him before he shows himself. Then in his perfect timing, he lovingly comes and reveals himself to us. That was what happened to Nancy. She was sitting on the edge of a canyon just above our small cabin when in desperation she asked God to make himself known to her. He honored her plea—and that was the day everything began to change.

Penetrating Truth

With the use of a battery-operated radio, Nancy began to spend her long days listening to Bible teachers like Charles Stanley, Chuck Smith, and James Dobson. She discovered if she earnestly prayed and sought God, he would not only minister to her but also make provision for her. The answer to one of those heartfelt prayers was an older couple who lived on the closest ranch a mile down the road. When Larry and Clara Pilgrim retired as foremen for the ranch owned by the Griffins, Ken and Jean Chaney took their place. They were strong Christians, and Jean, being an older woman, was a wonderful encouragement as she mentored and nurtured Nancy's hungering faith. Jean started taking Nancy with her to a Bible study in town once a week, and Nancy's faith began to grow rapidly.

This was also the beginning of some major stress in our marriage. I was wrapped up in my busy life. I was teaching school, raising a young family, and building a ranch. I was working hard trying to provide a good life for my new family. I was also becoming frustrated with Nancy's increasing unrest. She desperately wanted me to understand what she was experiencing, but I just couldn't seem to get it. As the sower parable implies, until the seed penetrates the hard soil, the truth makes no sense at all.

Meanwhile God began a season of deep healing in Nancy's wounded heart. Painful issues of her past began to surface as God continually and faithfully ministered his love and healing to her. This process took a while, and it also took a toll on our relationship. Healing can be an uncomfortable process and often impacts those around the one being healed, especially those who are closest and safest. I say all this because it was Nancy's healing process that allowed the seed of God's love to break through my own hardened heart.

More to keep peace than anything else, I started to take our family to church on Sunday mornings. I never had an aversion to church; in fact, I thought it was a wholesome thing for a young family to do. After all, I had been raised in church and I thought I had come out pretty well. Going to church was a respectable, responsible thing to do, and a good way to see your neighbors once a week.

The church we attended was called Chapel in the Pines. It was a small community church that literally began in a tent under a pine tree. I liked going at first because we could ride our horses to church and I could wear my spurs without seeming too conspicuous. On any given Sunday, about forty of us filed into the pews. Our pastor had come up from the city, feeling called to evangelism. He loved seeing people come to the Lord, but to his disappointment, most of the men who attended each Sunday were long ago saved or too stubborn and proud to consider giving him the satisfaction of raising our hands at his altar calls. In retrospect I think I always felt a little sorry for him; he probably felt like a failure at the time. Actually, though, most of us ended up giving our lives to Christ and serving in some form of ministry as well.

One Sunday our pastor announced that the Baptist church in the next community had invited all of our men to a weekend retreat. I decided to go along, and it was during this weekend that I finally realized salvation required a personal, willful decision. In a genuine act of surrender, I committed myself to God and went forward for prayer. I know that something very real happened to me that night, but it was only the embryo of a whole new life I was to experience in the years to come. I believe Christian maturity is a journey, but it is a journey that requires a first step. I had finally taken that first step.

Surrendering All

When I got home from that mountaintop weekend, I was excited to share with Nancy what had happened. This was the very thing that for many years she had desperately wanted and prayed for. In the years since she had invited Christ into her life on the side of the canyon, she had been praying for me every day.

> *I believe Christian maturity is a journey, but it is a journey that requires a first step.*

Proverbs 13:12 says, "Hope deferred makes the heart grow sick," and I believe that must have been what happened. I think Nancy was recovering from a sick heart after all those years of not having her prayers answered concerning me. For so long she had wanted me to become the spiritual leader of our home, and when it was about to happen, I think it was kind of a letdown for her. At first, she was elated, but her happiness soon turned to anger. She got mad and over the next couple of weeks, her anger became visible. I couldn't understand what was happening, and I remember wondering if receiving the Lord was such a good idea. I started to question everything about faith and this stimulated real and honest prayer—for the first time in my life.

It was during this time one Sunday after church that everything came to a head. Our young daughter, Katie, had gone to the home of some friends. The rest of us headed home for lunch, and our three-year-old son, Brook, went down for a nap. We had just met a new older couple at church that morning and had invited them to drop by later that day. Everything seemed fine until something snapped, and a fight between Nancy and me began. I don't know what started it or even what it was about, but I do remember it escalated rapidly. All at once everything came out—all of Nancy's anger and all of my frustration erupted, causing Nancy to pick up a pottery mug and hurl it at me across the room. I was able to duck quickly, and the mug missed me and smashed through the window of the front door.

As only fate would have it, the couple we invited from church arrived and were walking up the front steps at that very moment. They ducked and evaded the flying mug but decided it was not the best time to visit the Robinsons. They turned on their heels and headed for their car.

I was embarrassed and humiliated, and I lost it like I have never lost it before or since. I started yelling and hitting walls and cupboards. Framed pictures and dishes fell to the floor. I went from room to room turning over furniture and shouting in complete frustration. No matter how hard I tried, I couldn't make Nancy satisfied with our life, and I didn't know what I could do about it. In the wake of this realization, I fell apart.

All my life I had prided myself on being composed and put together; I always felt that showing emotion was a sign of weakness. That day God tore down everything I leaned on for strength. He was showing me that without him I would never be the person he created me to be. I needed him to be more than my Savior—I needed him to be the Lord of my life. That day I learned in my confession of weakness that he would make me strong (see 2 Cor. 12:10).

As I surveyed the aftermath of my rage, I saw my three-year-old son staring at me with huge, frightened eyes. I will never forget how he looked as he stood there in shock and disbelief. That's when it happened—that's when I finally broke. My deep frustration turned to tears, and the floodgates opened. I started to weep in a way I never had before. Tears welled up from the depths of my being, and my entire body started to convulse. I cried and cried and couldn't stop the tears. I cried for a whole life of pain and frustration, most of which Nancy had nothing to do with. I was broken in a way I can't fully express, but it was a brokenness that forever changed me. I held my son and Nancy held me, and together we cried and prayed. We repented for the way we had treated each other and together asked God to take control of our lives.

It was a divine moment in our marriage and a divine moment in our life with God. I believe it was the moment the seed of God's love and truth penetrated my life. It was a turning point, more powerful than any other I have ever experienced. My journey with God entered into the depths of good soil—to a place where my spiritual roots penetrated his provision for healing and wholeness. Not only did my relationship with God heal, my relationship with my wife changed as well. I could now love because I had come into the assurance that I was first loved.

The Gift of Repentance

Repentance is a gift from God. It is an essential ingredient prompted by faith that releases God's grace and ushers in Christ's provision for freedom. Repentance is the godly response to life's sorrow. Everyone has sorrow and regret; they are part of the human experience and there is no getting around them. It is not a matter of *if* you have sorrow and regret, because we all do at times in our lives. It is instead a matter of what you decide to do about them. Without repentance all sorrow ends in paralyzing regret, which if left unattended becomes a state of spiritual death.

> *Repentance is a gift from God.*

At one point when the apostle Paul was writing to the Corinthians, he explained this concept. He was telling them he was sorry he had rebuked them so strongly in his letter for not dealing with sin in the church in Corinth, but that he had been blessed by the way they responded to his correction. He wrote:

> Now I am glad I sent it, not because it hurt you, but because the pain caused you to repent and change your ways. It was the kind of sorrow God wants his people to have, so you were not harmed by us in any way. For the kind of sorrow God wants us to experience leads us away from sin and results in salvation. There's no regret for that kind of sorrow. But worldly sorrow, which lacks repentance, results in spiritual death.
>
> 2 Corinthians 7:9–10 NLT

In Jesus's parable of the sower, we understand that authentic Christian maturity happens only in good soil.

Though there is much to be learned about what makes soil good, the first thing to note is that it must be cultivated and broken to receive the seed. In the soil of the heart, this translates into authentic repentance. A heart broken through repentance is a place where faith can grow and produce fruit. For the person who has experienced true repentance, it becomes a way of life and not just another theological concept.

3

The Compost of Our Lives

Growing through the Pain

Many years after that turning point in our marriage, Nancy and I spent countless hours walking the hills and gullies of the land that would one day become our home at the base of Timber Butte in Idaho. We walked it in every season and at different times of the day, taking note of the snow depth in winter, the wet boggy spots in spring, and the position of the sun in summer and fall. We examined soil conditions and vegetation and we noted the places that were best protected from the high winds that frequented the exposed open hills. We didn't want to make a mistake when it came time to break ground to start our new farmstead, and it took a while before we could decide where that should be.

Eventually we chose a decomposed granite, knoblike hill in the center of the property. After hiring three experts with good reputations as water locators, it was determined that this particular knob would be the most probable place to hit water when it came time to drill a well. The knob would also provide a vantage point from which we could view most of the grazing land and be able to keep an eye on our livestock. And finally, it was the least fertile ground on the entire eighty acres. We wanted to save the most fertile land for hay production and free grazing pastures. In addition we felt it would be better to build a barn and house on granite rather than on clay that would turn to sticky mud in the rainy seasons. We were satisfied with our choice, but it had one shortfall: the soil where we would put our vegetable garden was decomposed granite like everything else close to the proposed house location, and it contained too little humus and nutrients to grow anything.

By the fall of 2007, we had contoured the granite knob into a two-acre landscape that would hold our new little farmstead. The foundation for the house had already been poured, and I had started construction on the pole barn that would take me more than a year to build.

It was a beautiful, warm fall day when we heard the rattling and clattering of an old dump truck laboring up our quarter-mile lane. As it rounded the corner, we could see heaped up on the bed a mountain of steaming, mucky cow manure. To us, it was a beautiful sight. Craig and Joan Krosh, our good neighbors from down the road, had been cleaning out their cattle pens in preparation for winter and decided to bless us with what turned out to be twelve heaping loads of fresh manure for our future vegetable garden. Their mountain of manure was the best housewarming present we had ever received.

The manure brewed under the snow all winter, its occasional smell reminding us that we would have to deal with it in the coming spring when the ground thawed and dried out. By April the air was warm and the land ready for us to work in the manure. Hooking a cultivator to the farm tractor, I spread the decomposed pile and turned it under until it was thoroughly mixed into the nonfertile earth beneath. Where there was once just dirt, the beginnings of soil now lay. It would one day nourish a garden and produce a bountiful harvest.

How God Works

Reflecting on Jesus's parable of the sower, the only soil where the seed managed to take permanent root was broken and fertile soil. It is ironic to realize that fertile soil is soil that has been composted with animal waste, rotted garbage, and microorganisms of every kind. Somehow God is able to do his best work in the depths of the compost of our lives.

> Somehow God is able to do his best work in the depths of the compost of our lives.

It is human nature to avoid pain at all costs. We hate it when we are faced with suffering, and yet it is often not until our faith is tested that our spiritual growth accelerates. I have always resisted the Scripture in James 1 that says, "When troubles come your way, consider it an opportunity for great joy. For you know that when your faith is tested, your endurance has a chance to grow. So let it grow, for when your endurance is fully developed, you will be perfect and complete, needing nothing" (vv. 2–4 NLT). Another

Scripture I've steered clear of is in Romans where Paul told the people, "We can rejoice, too, when we run into problems and trials, for we know that they help us develop endurance. And endurance develops strength of character, and character strengthens our confident hope of salvation" (Rom. 5:3–4 NLT).

As a pastor I have watched many children grow up in good Christian homes with parents who have done everything in their power to insulate them from the pain, suffering, and dysfunction of the world. Yet when many of these kids enter into young adulthood, they have a tendency to become apathetic in their faith. This isn't true in every case, but it happens quite often. On the flip side, I have watched as some who have been in the gutter of drug abuse, broken families, and major life crises come to Christ and embrace Christian growth, and then later are powerfully used by the Lord to help set others free.

When we think of Christianity, we like to think about the end product—a life that demonstrates biblical truth, productive ministry, and the manifestation of the fruits of the Spirit. We often fail to recognize that these characteristics usually come only after a very long and difficult journey.

Brook's Story

About a year after establishing our new farmstead in the mountains of Idaho, I accepted a speaking engagement that took me to San Diego. Because of it, I was away from home for several days. My flight to Boise arrived late at night, and I was ready to be back in my own bed. Our ranch is about an hour out of town. I had just paid the parking fee and started on the long trek home when my cell phone rang. It was our son, Brook, and he sounded distressed.

Brook, who is in his early thirties, is an avid extreme sports enthusiast. Two years earlier he had experienced a skiing accident that badly damaged his jaw joint. After many hours of painful therapy, his doctors finally advised him to undergo surgery that would require breaking his jaw joint and having his mouth wired shut for a minimum of eight weeks. He had undergone the surgery a week before I left on my ministry trip, and when I heard him that night on the phone, I felt certain the pain in his voice was related to his recovery. It wasn't. He was talking through wired teeth, and at first I couldn't understand what he was trying to say. Then I got it. He told me his wife of seven years had just informed him she was leaving him for good. He was in shock and I was in disbelief. As far as I knew, they had a good marriage. They did everything together, and I had never seen them fight. I was dumbfounded.

As only the Lord would have it, when we ended our phone conversation, I was just a few minutes from Brook's house. When I got there, our daughter was with him. We talked for quite a while as Brook struggled to fill in the details. Though it seemed unbelievable at the time, it was all true: Brook's wife had really left him. In the midst of the most extreme emotional pain Brook had ever experienced in his life, he was at a ground zero of physical pain as well. I knew Brook was a strong person, but this was the greatest test of his life. Though many times I have walked people through suffering and pain in my professional life as a pastor, that night I had no words for my son. I felt helpless; I could only tell him how sorry I was. Together we prayed for him, not knowing what else we could do.

Brook's physical condition was serious. He had to be continually monitored, especially in the night. With his wife out of the picture, Nancy and I brought Brook home for this period of recovery. The next month was one of the most difficult times any of us have ever experienced. Brook's emotional pain exacerbated his physical injury. In his sleep at night, Brook would unconsciously clench his teeth, which would reinjure his jaw. Because of his pain medication, he had to constantly fight nausea, and one day he continually vomited through his teeth. In the middle of this painful recovery, his wife presented him with divorce papers and wanted everything finalized.

We all have times when we are waist deep in the muck. Sometimes life just stinks.

Before all this happened, Brook had slowly drifted out of close relationship not only with us but with the Lord. As a young child he had a fervent faith, and as a teenager he had some amazing experiences with the Lord and with ministry. As a family we had spent significant time among the hill tribes of Burma and Thailand; and while he was in high school, Brook had gone with me down the Amazon and up the Shingo River ministering to villages along the way.

In his younger days, Brook had experienced and seen the power of the Lord. As an adult he had become busy with life and engaged in recreational sports of all kinds. He was respected in his profession and was also a responsible, loving husband. Brook had always been a good person, but in the last few years, it felt as if we had lost meaningful relationship with him. We rarely saw him at church on Sundays due to his work schedule, and we were left to wonder where he was in his faith. In the midst of his excruciating pain and suffering, things began to change.

During those days and nights of recovery, Brook couldn't drive because of the strong pain medication he was on. He was literally stuck at the ranch with little to do but write and talk—and he did both profusely. He chronicled all he was going through, telling his whole story—a sad story but also one of extreme transparency and honesty. He spoke of his suffering, but more than that he spoke of all he was learning about himself; he was candid about his strengths as well as his deficits. Every night we would talk for hours, and Nancy and I were constantly amazed at Brook's perspective on life and the maturity he displayed as he made crucial decisions about his future. The season of pain and suffering was a time of divine growth for Brook. He restored relationships that had waned, with us and with the Lord.

Not only did Brook experience growth, but through his suffering and our participation in it, we did as well. In the end, a peace permeated our entire family and the joy of our being together was restored. Holidays were a rich time once again. God turned a devastating season into something rich, meaningful, and good. Now, looking back, Brook has professed that despite the pain and heartache, he would willingly live through his ordeal again for the growth he experienced because of it.

Six months later, Brook was working in his vegetable garden preparing it for spring planting when a revelation concerning his winter of pain and anguish came to him. He wrote a blog post that evening for all his friends to read:

Entry #9—Spring

The other day I was out in my yard preparing my garden for the upcoming season. Earlier that day, my sister and I had picked up a truckload of compost, and I was working it deep into the soil. As I stopped and looked around me, the signs of spring were everywhere. My apple trees were budding, the cherry tree was blooming, and as I stood there, it hit me that my soul was at peace. It has been six months since my wife left, and in that time I have experienced more of what life can throw at you than I care to remember, but life has returned. New buds are forming around me, and each one is more significant and valued due to those experiences. I can see life for what it is and I can feel more deeply. For the first time in a long time I can breathe life in—I feel like one of the buds on my apple trees—reaching out for the sun after a long period of dormancy. It was an inert state I was in long before she left—one that I fell into—unaware of the slow slide. My life was sad, self-focused, and unfulfilled. I'm not saying that everything is perfect now, but life is rich. I still have anger issues with her, and I probably will for a long time to come. I continue to have moments where I fear abandonment from those I love, but those feelings are unfounded, and will pass—I know this. All of this is to say that these experiences will follow me, but time dulls the edges and with spring—life returns.

There are certain aspects of the past 24 weeks that I wouldn't trade for the world. New friendships have been kindled, and some old ones have been restored. One in particular has come—quite suddenly and unexpectedly. I had told myself that I wasn't going to see anyone for a year, but if these experiences have taught me anything, it is that my self-made plans never seem to work out. She first came to me with words of encouragement when I had no courage and with a message of hope when I had little optimism. She came as a simple friend, but that friendship has grown and taken root in my life. She is someone I respect for her character, admire for her fortitude, and love for her tenderness. Some may feel that too little time has passed, but there are times in one's life when not accepting that gift that has been given would be foolish and forever regretted—she is such a gift.

It is amazing to see the twists and turns the path of life can present. Even now it is hard to wrap my mind around this period of my life, but I am grateful for the outcome thus far. I don't need to tell you where compost comes from, but out of that compost comes fertility and the foundation for new growth. Without it new life could not establish itself, and desolation would take over. I am thankful for the compost in my life—not for the making, but for the growth that comes out of it. It has been a time that I hope to never again experience but I wouldn't change it. I wouldn't go back and dull the pain, or arrest the free fall. At this point, I value each new breath and I look forward to the upcoming season.

The Nature of God

When we find ourselves in a season where we are living in the compost heap, it is often difficult to see God's presence in the midst of it. Yet it has been my experience that he's not only there but there most powerfully. It is God's desire and very nature to restore lives.

> *I am thankful for the compost in my life—not for the making, but for the growth that comes out of it.*

Not long ago I was sitting in my study preparing for the Easter message I was to preach the following Sunday. After the winter we had experienced with Brook, and in the midst of a disabling economy that had snatched away so many jobs of those in our church, I wanted

51

desperately to bring a message that was real and relevant for the moment. My brain seemed stuck that morning as I sat there looking at my blank computer screen.

Then I felt the prompting of the Lord to get up and cross my study to the west-facing window. In reluctant obedience I got up and looked. What I saw changed my thinking immediately. The light of a new day was breaking on a distant butte, illuminating the inbreak of spring. It caused something to leap in my spirit when I realized the last of the long winter snow was melting rapidly and the land that had been dormant for so long was about to explode into new life again. It was a revealing picture of the nature of God, and in that moment I felt the Lord say to me, *Go tell the people that my nature is for resurrection.*

Our God is a God of restoration, reconciliation, renewal, new beginnings. He is the God of second chances, healing, deliverance, and freedom. He turns darkness to glorious light. He is the God of resurrection. Consider how a seed dies at the end of one season and falls into the ground, giving birth to new life as the new season breaks forth. Consider how a prairie fire scorches the land, turning everything in its path into ashes, only to bring forth greener and healthier grasslands as the rains fall and the new season begins.

When the prophet Isaiah spoke of God's intentions for the coming Messiah, he told us he would be in the business of replacing ashes for a crown of beauty, of turning mourning into a joyous blessing, of turning despair into festive praise (Isa. 61:1–3). God desires to rebuild cities and lives that have been destroyed and to turn shame and dishonor into a double share of honor. Isaiah said that

God's righteousness would be like a garden in early spring, with plants springing up everywhere (61:11). This is the heart and intention of God for all humanity; it is his desire to make all things new for any who dare to embrace his provision.

Jesus said, "In the world you have tribulation and trials and distress and frustration; but be of good cheer [take courage; be confident, certain, undaunted]! For I have overcome the world. [I have deprived it of power to harm you and have conquered it for you.]" (John 16:33 AMP). It is a promise to us! It is not a matter of *if* we will experience troubles and difficulty in our lives; it is a matter of what we will do when those inevitable bad things happen.

For years I have heard Christians quote Paul's encouraging statement: "And we know that God causes everything to work together for the good . . ." neglecting to finish the end of the sentence: "of those who love God and are called according to his purpose for them" (Rom.

> *If we choose to receive God's love for us (and love him for it in return) and desire to embrace his purpose for us, his promise is to reach down into the compost pile, take our hand, and raise us up.*

8:28 NLT). In other words, God turns bad things into good things, sometimes even great things, for those who embrace his provision for resurrection. He died on the cross and was resurrected on the third day for the forgiveness of our sins. Sin interferes, interrupts, and stops God's outstretched hand of restoration. He wants to turn it around for us, but by our own free will we can reject or accept his intervention. If we choose to receive his love for us (and love him for it in return) and desire to embrace his purpose for us, his promise is to reach down into the compost pile, take our hand, and raise us up.

I want to be a person who will always look for the blessing—even in the darkest, smelliest seasons of my life. I think God works things for good for those who expect him to because they have come to trust in his character and nature. Sometimes I wish it were different, but I have come to realize that seeds cannot grow in sterile soil; they need compost and manure to be nourished for what might one day become a great harvest.

4

The Planted Seed

God's Hidden Work

More than ten years ago I bought my first real tractor. It wasn't much to look at, but it was a bona fide Allis Chalmers 1952 D17 farm tractor and it ran great. The guy who sold it to me was a gentleman rancher who wanted something a little more modern and easier to use. The tractor came with all kinds of implements: a disc, two mowers, a harrow, a plow, a scraper blade, and a number of other miscellaneous pieces of farm equipment. I was elated with so many new toys, even though I knew little about how to use them.

Though the tractor was worn from years of use and sometimes temperamental, it served me well. The most difficult thing about it was that it was very hard to steer. To my knowledge it had never been equipped with power steering, and operating it in close quarters around the house or barn was a challenge. When I had a load in the bucket, the extra weight on the front tires made it nearly impossible to turn unless the tractor was moving. On days that I used the tractor a lot, I would get muscle soreness in my chest and arms as though I had been weight lifting at the gym. It wore me out.

Not long ago a friend named Tom Gatfield came over to help me do some work on the ranch here at Timber Butte. I was using the old tractor to move some empty fuel tanks while he stood off at a short distance watching me. As I lifted one of them with the bucket and started maneuvering it to another location, he saw how I strained to turn the steering wheel. I couldn't help but notice a curious and somewhat bewildered expression on his face. As I set the tank down, he yelled over the noise of the engine, "What's wrong with that tractor of yours?"

I shouted back, "It doesn't have power steering."

Tom had been raised with tractors and large farm equipment; their mechanics was second nature to him. He tilted his head as if to have a closer look at my old Allis Chalmers, and being careful not to make me feel totally stupid, he simply said, "Are you familiar with how to fill your power-steering reservoir?"

Turning off the engine, I answered, "I didn't even know it had one."

Tom showed me how to remove the front grill and locate a small filler tube I had never seen before. Later that day I drove it up to my shop and poured nearly two gallons of tractor hydraulic fluid down the small opening, replaced the cap, and started up the engine. It took a few minutes for things to start working, but I had power steering. It changed everything! It was like I had a whole new tractor, and I didn't know how to respond. On one hand I was elated at my discovery, but at the same time I was mad because I had been struggling with it for more than ten years. I was upset because it had never occurred to me that the luxury of power steering was an option.

Living without God in our lives is like my tractor experience. We can steer our way through life on our own power if we want to, or we can fill our tank with God's Spirit and let him shoulder the burden. Often when people discover the power of the Holy Spirit later rather than sooner, they react as I did when Tom told me to fill up the power-steering reservoir. They are filled with joy at the discovery but may be frustrated it took them so long. Now I realize I had become so accustomed to struggling to steer my tractor that I thought it couldn't be any different. I had no idea there was a better way. I hadn't thought to ask if there was a hidden truth I didn't know. Maybe I was just too proud.

Every human being is equipped with a power reservoir, but it needs to be filled, which is what God does in us when we come to him in faith. As Paul said in his letter to his "son in the faith" Titus, "When God our Savior revealed his kindness and love, he saved us, not because of the righteous things we had done, but because of his mercy. He washed away our sins, giving us a new birth and new life through the Holy Spirit. He generously poured out the Spirit upon us through Jesus Christ our Savior" (Titus 3:4–6 NLT). The trouble is, we forget this. We take the wheel in our own hands, with our own strength, and just keep steering hard, trying to make everything work. To be filled with God's presence is an ongoing choice for us, and it's often a repeated discovery process as well, found only in the struggle of trying to live without it.

A Mystery

After his analogy of the sower recorded in Mark 4, Jesus spoke a second time about the miracle that takes place in the good soil, saying:

> This is what the kingdom of God is like. A man scatters seed on the ground. Night and day, whether he sleeps or gets up, the seed sprouts and grows, though he does not know how. All by itself the soil produces grain—first the stalk, then the head, then the full kernel in the head. As soon as the grain is ripe, he puts the sickle to it, because the harvest has come.
>
> Mark 4:26–29

During the time of waiting, the seed is hidden, visible only to God. It is during this waiting period that the hard protective outer shell of the seed begins to soften so that its first fragile root can break out and tap into the rich nourishment of the earth. This mysterious work is done out of the sight and control of man, and what takes place is nothing short of miraculous. This part of the growth process must be completed before the immature plant can break forth from its place of confinement, sending out the first shoots. As they break through to the surface, the tiny plant finally announces its existence and is observed and recognized as a new and unique creation.

The same kind of process must also take place in us. If we, like the seed, are to grow fully into a new creation, we must undergo God's essential and miraculous work—which is often hidden from view—in unexpected and even uncomfortable seasons of life. For most this is a confusing time, a time when we question if God even knows us or cares about what we are going through. Sometimes it's a dark time of trials, a lonely place where we feel trapped and without human options; yet it is the very place God seems to do his best work in us. It's here that we finally give up and choose to surrender to his will.

When Jesus shared the parable of the sower and the soils, he said, "And the seeds that fell on the good soil represent honest, good-hearted people who hear God's word, cling to it, and patiently produce a huge harvest" (Luke 8:15 NLT). In a first pass through this portion of Scripture, it may sound so simple, yet there is one word that many of us would rather overlook: *patiently*. Patience is something few American Christians can accept or tolerate very well. Living in a culture that demands fast service and excellent quality, we expect to get the things we want immediately with no waiting; we expect all our desires to be gratified and satisfied promptly. We have translated the expectations that come with living in a fast-food, Internet society to our Christian experience.

When Paul said in Romans 12:2 that we are no longer to conform to the pattern of the world, he was talking about transforming our worldview to a new upside-down-

> *If we, like the seed, are to grow fully into a new creation, we must undergo God's essential and miraculous work—which is often hidden from view—in unexpected and even uncomfortable seasons of life.*

kingdom view. This transformation may be one of the greatest miracles we experience because our perspectives on life have been ingrained from birth by a lifetime of experiences, good and bad. Without the sovereign hand of God, however, these perspectives may never truly be changed or transformed. This miraculous yet tedious process of transformation can happen only in the depths of the good soil. As we surrender ourselves to the deeper work of God, we find we are covered in his love during this time of development. Because we are often slow to learn, this process requires time and therefore patience on our part.

A Miracle

On the ranch in early spring, only a few varieties of vegetables can be planted in preparation for the summer harvest. One of these early crops is lettuce. When going through the process of preparing the ground for the new season, we till it and mix in compost. Then it's time to plant the first seeds of spring. I don't know if you have ever planted lettuce, but I will attest to the fact that the seeds are so small, they are nearly microscopic. The instructions on the seed packet say to plant each seed half an inch deep and two to four inches apart in cultivated rich soil. Seriously, for a sixty-one-year-old guy who needs glasses to read numbers in a phone book, there is no good way to do this. My best effort is to make a small shallow trench and randomly sprinkle seeds into it.

For the life of me I can't understand how something so small can grow into an eight- to ten-inch head of lettuce. Anyone who denies the existence of a creative Designer behind this one very small part of creation just hasn't had any cognitive experience living in nature. Even the tiniest seeds are a great miracle.

Jesus talked a lot about seeds when he was teaching about being transformed and growing in his kingdom. In Matthew 13, he communicated this point concerning how something very small can produce something very amazing when he said, "The Kingdom of Heaven is like a mustard seed planted in a field. It is the smallest of all seeds, but it becomes the largest of garden plants; it grows into a tree, and birds come and make nests in its branches" (vv. 31–32 NLT). He also said that if a seed is to produce a great harvest, the first thing it must do is die and be planted in soil. He put it this way: "I tell you the truth, unless a kernel of wheat is planted in the soil and dies, it remains alone. But its death will produce many new kernels—a plentiful harvest of new lives" (John 12:24 NLT). If real maturity and fruitfulness are to be produced in and through our lives, two things must happen. First, we must die to ourselves; and second, we must submit ourselves to a long, deep, and transforming process that allows God to rebuild us into his new creation.

Planting a small seed requires pushing it down into rich soil completely out of sight. Literally the seed is put into a place where it is invisible to the eye for a season of time. No one enjoys the feeling of being invisible; it goes against all human nature. In our humanness we want to feel significant and noticed. We want more than anything to be recognized for the things we do, no matter how small they may be. Yet God seems to do his best work when he has us in hiding—in a place where our efforts may even go unnoticed.

After having an amazing conversion experience on the road to Damascus, the apostle Paul was baptized and healed by an obedient disciple named Ananias. Like so many young Christians, Paul immediately wanted to share his newfound faith with everyone, especially his old Jewish friends. They knew he had come to Damascus to persecute Christians and take them away in chains. It was only two chapters earlier in the book of Acts that Paul stood affirming the execution of Stephen, the first martyr of the church. If his Jewish friends had heard about his conversion, they must have been totally confused.

Paul's new zeal to preach the gospel didn't bear any fruit that we are aware of; instead, he had to flee the city for fear of losing his life. Although there is no detailed record of what happened, Scripture tells us Paul spent the next three years in the desert of Arabia after which time he returned to Jerusalem. On his arrival there he tried to build relationships with the original apostles, but they sent him away to his hometown of Tarsus, where he spent about a decade hidden away (at least from our eyes) until Barnabas decided to go find him. Only after that did he begin what we generally view as his public ministry. Paul was seemingly invisible for perhaps a decade or more. He was a seed buried for a very long season of time before he broke ground and became a plant that ultimately produced a magnificent harvest.

Those hidden years were probably the most essential and significant in the development of Paul's new life in Christ. He was like a seed that died to his own worldview and was taken underground to be transformed and resurrected into a vessel that God would one day use very powerfully.

Here is the question: What can God do in us when he puts us in a hidden place that he cannot do in public?

Growth Rhythms and Timing

When Nancy and I were first married and living on the old family ranch in California, we found ourselves in need of money. We wanted to build an addition onto our small cabin but didn't have the resources to do it. Even though we had a very simple lifestyle, my new teacher's salary of seven hundred dollars a month barely met our needs. It was during this time that my dad made a proposal to us that would give us a little extra cash.

He had the idea of starting a pine tree nursery there on the ranch. He offered to underwrite the initial costs if we would pay him back after the trees reached maturity and were sold to landscapers. It was a great offer, but we had no idea how to turn a small pine nut into a sellable pine tree. With a little investigation Nancy discovered a class that was being offered at a Forest Service tree plantation not far from us, and she decided to sign up. With the knowledge and experience she gained from the class as well as working in the plantation, we were able to begin this new venture. Armed with youthful expectation and a basic understanding of what we had to do, we purchased our first batch of seed and made preparations to plant a thousand trees.

When the first package of pine nuts arrived in the mail, we placed them in a large jar of wet peat moss and put them in the freezer for several weeks. This part of the process, we were told, was called stratification. The work of stratification is important, as it artificially sets a God-given clock within the anatomy of seeds as if to alert and prepare them for explosive growth in the warmth of spring and summer. You might say stratification puts the seeds in touch with the rhythms and timing of God's plan. Somehow it simulates the dormancy of winter and synchronizes the timing for the seeds so they all break open and shoot out a taproot at the perfect time.

One of the powerful things God desires to do in us during our time of spiritual invisibility or dormancy is to get us in touch with his rhythms and timing. He wants us to understand how important his timing is and the necessity of coming to a place where we flow naturally in his rhythms. He is a God of changing seasons and we must learn to be patient and attuned to the ebb and flow of his Spirit. He wants us to learn how important it is not to get ahead of him and operate in our own human power. Also, he doesn't want us to become apathetic and fall behind him, missing his open doors and divine opportunities. The season of stratification is one in which we are positioned to sit quietly and learn to discern his voice.

Stratification is not something that can easily happen during the hectic busyness of a public life of ministry. It happens more readily during wilderness times like that of Paul in the desert of Arabia. The stratification or wilderness time provides a period to learn about the heart, character, and nature of God. Nearly every biblical hero of the faith experienced it. Abraham, Jacob, Moses, David, John the Baptist—they all did their wilderness time. Even Jesus spent time in the wilderness before he entered his three years of public ministry.

As for Paul and his time in the desert, I suspect God took him out of ministry to save him from himself, knowing that in his spiritual immaturity he could do more harm than good. God had a big plan for Paul, and because of it he wanted to take Paul through his heavenly school of preparation. Paul learned huge lessons during this invisible season. He learned he could be content while on center stage, which he was for much of his adult life, or while being hidden and confined. Some of Paul's most effective ministry and writing took place in a jail cell. It was there that he wrote, "I have learned the secret of being content in any and every situation, whether well fed or hungry, whether living in plenty or in want. I can do everything through him who gives me strength" (Phil. 4:12–13).

Active Faith

Shortly after I gave my life to the Lord, Nancy wanted us to attend a new church that had recently been planted in Lancaster, California, which was about an hour from our ranch. I admit I was reluctant for a couple reasons. First, I didn't want to spend two hours driving on a Sunday morning going to and from church. The other fact that fueled my hesitancy was that this particular church had been birthed out of the Jesus Movement of the seventies and had a reputation for being very nontraditional and even radical. I just assumed it was primarily made up of a bunch of born-again, Jesus-freak hippies who had come to Jesus after smoking too much marijuana in the sixties. You might say I had a bad attitude, but to keep peace in our home, I went, reluctantly. Obviously at the time I had

65

no idea this would be the body of believers that would launch us into a whole new life of ministry.

The church was called the Desert Vineyard and was affiliated with a fast-growing network of new churches called Calvary Chapel. They met in a cold, unattractive concrete structure that was part of the county fairgrounds on the outskirts of town. The minute I walked through the door, I felt like a fish out of water. Though I was in my late twenties at the time, I felt middle-aged compared to the others in the room.

A girl with long black hair sat on a bar stool perched on a crudely made plywood stage. She was softly strumming a guitar while leading the roomful of participants in singing. As I recall, the first thought that entered my mind was that we had accidentally walked into a Joan Baez concert. But I couldn't deny that I experienced something that touched a deep place in me. This church was made up of people from every walk of life, mostly young with a smattering of older folks. I identified some as bikers and cowboys, and some I labeled normal folks (*like me*). Everyone was engaged in the act of worship, and each person seemed to be unaware that anyone else was in the room. It was amazing, and as hard as I tried to resist, I couldn't help being drawn into what I would now label an authentic Christian church.

The pastor's name was Brent Rue; he was a zealous, creative young man in his early thirties. He exemplified the leadership that rose out of the Jesus Movement. Laid-back, very intelligent, a great communicator, funny at times, he was deeply passionate about discipleship. Brent was six feet seven inches tall and a man to be looked up to, not only because of his physical stature but also because of his personal example.

Brent and his wife, Happy, were looking for a place not too far out of town to do a one-day discipleship getaway, so we invited them to take a look at our ranch. When we described our place to them, it seemed to be exactly what they needed. Brent and Happy drove out to look over our home, and Nancy invited them to stay for dinner. That spontaneous invitation changed the course of our lives forever, as God began to develop a growing relationship between the Rues and us.

It was around this time that Brent met a man called Brother Andrew, who had written a book about his experiences smuggling Bibles into Russia and China. He called the book *God's Smuggler* and told about the underground church in both countries. Brent was so stirred by his compelling story that he decided the church in Lancaster had to become involved. He had already recruited two men in the fellowship to join Brother Andrew's quest to secretly transport Bibles into Communist China. This was in the late seventies when China's borders had just opened to tourists for the first time in many years. Mao Tse-Tung, the famous Communist dictator, had died recently, and the new regime decided to loosen China's borders in an effort to gain international favor.

Yet Christianity was outlawed in China, and citizens were forbidden to own Bibles. One of the two men Brent sent on the first venture had been caught, interrogated, and deported before he even entered the country. But in the midst of persecution there had been a growing underground revival going on. Some say more Christians were martyred in China during Mao's rule than there were Jewish people executed under Hitler's Nazi regime. The church in China was invisible, just like the lettuce seeds in our garden.

We heard about all of this at dinner that night. We talked for a long time about Brent's ambitious plan to transport thousands of Bibles into China. I was amazed that an American church would consider such a courageous ministry, and I said so. I'll never forget how Brent looked across our dining room table and asked me matter-of-factly, "Do you want to go?" It was almost as if he were asking me to pass the salt or something. I was so shocked that I spoke before I had time to think, and that small three-letter word *yes* somehow escaped from my mouth. Everything in me wanted to take it back immediately, but it was out there, and Brent quickly closed the deal by telling me he had an airline ticket that had to be used in two weeks. Because I was a schoolteacher on my summer break, I was free to go. Miraculously I was able to obtain my first passport, get a visa, get baptized in our old swimming hole, and be on an airplane only two weeks later.

It was crazy, but everything was a little crazy during those days of the Jesus Movement. The rules all changed, and normal everyday Christians had opportunities to do things that were life changing. Brent was the person who taught me that the word *Christianity* was meant to be a verb. We had to be active.

Ready to Grow

Experiencing the underground church inside China in 1979 was without a doubt the most life-altering experience I've had. I was never the same after that. For the first time in my life, I met truly invisible people—Chinese Christians who, like the seeds in my garden, were lying dormant underground for a season in preparation for a great harvest.

Before my trip to China, I had never left the comfort and security of the United States, except for a couple of short trips over the Mexican border. That realization alone made me feel a bit uneasy, plus the fact that I was about to smuggle illegal contraband into a Communist country. All bravado was gone, and I recognized my only hope was God. I realize now that it was the first time in my life I had experienced the feeling of having no other option than to put all my trust in him.

It started the minute Mark Van Gilder, my fellow smuggler, and I landed in Hong Kong. In those days they didn't have Jetways from the terminal to the plane, and we had to depart down a portable stairway out onto the tarmac. When the door of our 747 finally opened after twenty-four endless hours of travel, the smells and humidity of Hong Kong smacked me in the face like a wave. I remember thinking, *We're not in Kansas anymore, Toto.*

Over the next two days, Mark and I walked the streets of Hong Kong and met with a Chinese team that prepared us for the border crossing. We met a woman known as Mama Quang who had escaped from Mainland China a few years before with her family. Both she and her husband had been leaders in the underground church and suffered horrible persecution because of it. She had been put in a cell the size of a large animal cage for three years, and her husband had been buried up to his neck in sand for several days at a time. During these times of incarceration, their children were left to survive on their own with strict orders given by the Chinese Red Guard that no one was permitted to intervene. Meeting this courageous woman left a lasting impression on me.

We were invited to attend a church meeting late one night that included many more who had experienced similar persecution. Even though they were somewhat safe in Hong Kong, they remained underground when they gathered. That night we packed into a small confined room with about a hundred Chinese in 90 percent humidity and no air-conditioning. Mama Quang preached for an hour, and the people worshiped for another hour. I couldn't understand a word of the service itself, but afterward with the help of an interpreter I heard many compelling stories about these brave Christians that shook me to the core.

The next day we departed for the Mainland and managed to get our Bibles across the border and into the hands of our contact. We stayed in China for several days, and I truly fell in love with this very special group of Chinese Christians. Because the border had so recently been opened to the outside world, we white American tourists were quite a novelty. I was very aware that I had been given the special privilege of being raised in a country that allowed its people the freedom to pursue and openly worship God. My trip to China awakened me to the fact that I had taken it all for granted.

China's populated streets were jammed with people, all walking or riding bicycles. The only vehicles I saw were government trucks transporting soldiers and goods of every kind. The high-rise structures in the city were made out of concrete, and nothing was painted. The entire atmosphere was one of drab, depressing gray, yet the smiles and laughter of the people melted my heart. I didn't know it then, but a seed was planted in me during that experience. It began to mature as the hard shell of my heart fell away forever, and my roots longed to sink deep into the depths of God's truth. I needed to understand God's love for the Chinese people and what he felt about me. I wanted to know his plans for my life. I was ready to grow.

Some amazing things happened when I returned home, changes that both empowered and motivated me for a life that would eventually become one of full-time Christian service. China shook my worldview.

Wanting to Be Noticed

This was another season of brokenness for me—different from when Nancy's and my relationship fell to pieces and then healed. This time I got in touch with the heart of God for a people who had been broken and held captive. I fell in love in a whole new way as I experienced a small taste of the kind of love God has for humanity, the kind of love that motivates sacrifice. I was broken for the Chinese people but also because I had taken my own freedom for granted.

It hit me that for my entire life I had had access to a Bible but had never taken the time to read it. The fact that I had just smuggled several hundred Bibles to a group of people who were willing to risk their lives to own one, and that I had never even read the book, completely devastated me. I was so convicted I made the decision to go underground myself, so to speak, taking the truth of God's Word with me for a long season of time.

71

In the days and months that followed, I took every opportunity I could to read the study Bible Nancy gave me shortly after I was saved. In Luke 8 Jesus said that the seed in the parable of the sower represented God's Word; it is the truth about who God is and about his plan for humanity. Now this seed was becoming a part of me, and I spent hours hidden away, allowing it to penetrate deep into my heart so that it would impact my life.

The fact that I had just smuggled several hundred Bibles to a group of people who were willing to risk their lives to own one, and that I had never even read the book, completely devastated me.

It was during this time of my being hidden away, invisible, that God tested the motives of my heart. I think he was checking my progress to see if I was ready to break ground and enter the next phase of my Christian development. In those days I had become very involved in our ministry to China. We started to aggressively train and send small teams over to Hong Kong, where we had a full-time contact who arranged the transports across the border. Hong Kong was still independent from China, and Americans were free to come and go at will. To help send our people, we decided to raise money to pay half their airfare and travel expenses. Brent had the idea of collecting and selling used newspapers for recycling to raise the money.

We began to implement this idea of recycling newspapers, and we were so successful at it that we managed to raise thousands of dollars over a period of about three years. The only problem was that it took a massive amount of work, and all of it had to be done by volunteers. I was one of those volunteers, and every Sunday after church I took my family to a large retirement complex to do a weekly pickup. We would drive two vehicles to church each Sunday, my truck and our family car. The retirement center was on our way home, so we all would work for about two hours going from building to building picking up the papers that the folks had graciously saved for us. Every Sunday we would fill the bed of my truck with papers. Then Nancy would take the kids home, while I returned to church to empty the truck into a storage shelter.

Doing the job was okay for a while, but after several months it started to get old. Usually there were people at the church to help, but one time I distinctly remember unloading my truck back at church all by myself. It was hard, unpleasant work, and it was a cold, windy afternoon. I was about halfway through when the thought hit me that I really wasn't having fun and I felt all alone and very unappreciated. I wanted to be noticed; I wanted more than anything else for Brent to drive by and see me laboring away at his stupid fund-raising idea. I was tired of no one knowing I had been doing this job week after week for months. I hated being invisible and I wanted to quit. I threw down a bundle of papers and plopped on top of the growing pile of what seemed a lot like trash. That's when I prayed a prayer of complaint to the Lord, saying, "Please, Jesus, I just want someone to notice me."

And that's when Jesus answered me in his still, small but very clear voice, saying, *I do notice you, Tri. You're not invisible to me.* It wasn't that he was upset with me or rebuking me; it was just a matter-of-fact but tender comment.

Looking back after all these years (more than thirty now), I believe that single event may have had more to do with my future fruitfulness in public ministry than anything else. We may chafe at being invisible when everything in us wants to be seen and appreciated, but until we learn we are always in full view of God—and that's enough—our lives will never produce a harvest.

God not only sees us but loves us and wants the best for us. It is when we are planted deep in the soil of God's love that we can shoot a taproot like that tiny pine nut into the love of God. Paul's prayer over the church in Ephesus says it so well:

> I pray that from his glorious, unlimited resources he will empower you with inner strength through his Spirit. Then Christ will make his home in your hearts as you trust in him. Your roots will grow down into God's love and keep you strong. And may you have the power to understand, as all God's people should, how wide, how long, how high, and how deep his love is. May you experience the love of Christ, though it is too great to understand fully. Then you will be made complete with all the fullness of life and power that comes from God.
>
> Ephesians 3:16–19 NLT

Galatians
1:2

5

Soil, Sun, and Rain

A Picture of the Trinity

I love living where I can experience the changing seasons. Each season has special characteristics that distinguish it from another, and at the base of Timber Butte, where we live, it seems as though the seasons' defining qualities are heightened. The elevation here is higher than any place we have lived before, and because the country is so wide open, it is exposed to the harshness and severity of the changing weather season by season. The summers are hot and even dangerously dry, as the grass-covered hills become vulnerable to passing lightning storms and microbursts of wind that often accompany them.

Fall is incredibly beautiful with its changing colors. The crisp chill of the air brings a reminder to cut more firewood and store more hay and food in preparation for the confinement that the deep snows of the approaching winter will certainly bring.

Of all the seasons, I love spring the most. Spring beckons us to come outside and into the garden and orchard to witness firsthand the freshness of new life. The warming air freshened by spring rain is cleansing and invigorating, and together the air and rain transform the hills and pastures from a dormant winter brown to a rich deep green, as the cycle of life is seen in the changes of every growing thing.

As I write this chapter, it is spring on the homestead. After the long, confining winter, Nancy and I were both ready for a change. Just yesterday I came in from the garden declaring that the peas had broken ground. They were the first of the seeds we planted in mid-April, and they sprouted sooner than I had expected. New seasons are like new beginnings, especially when it comes to the season of spring.

I believe spring may be the most invigorating season, because it is like witnessing the miracle of a second chance. Jesus referred to this when he spoke to Nicodemus, the Pharisee, in John 3, explaining to him what it meant to be reborn of the Spirit or to be "born again." In John 12 Jesus gave a more organic reference when he said, "I tell you the truth, unless a kernel of wheat is planted in the soil and dies, it remains alone. But its death will produce many new kernels—a plentiful harvest of new lives. Those who love their life in this world will lose it. Those who care nothing for their life in this world will keep it for eternity" (John 12:24–25 NLT).

Yesterday as I witnessed those first sprouting peas, I saw something I don't recall having noticed before. Each little sprout was at a somewhat different stage in its young development. They all had established a root that penetrated into the soil to extract nourishment to strengthen and support the growth that was now evident. But on closer observation, I realized some were just breaking out from the confines of the earth, while others were in full upright positions. It looked as though some were in a bowed position and others were rising into an upright stance, spreading their small, fragile shoots upward as if in a posture of charismatic worship. It occurred to me that these small plants had been programmed to stretch out their first tiny leaves to gather light and warmth from the sun's rays and to grow upward into the brightness of the full day. I had somehow missed it before, but I am certain that what was going on in my garden is exactly what God intends for all who are reborn in him.

> *What was going on in my garden is exactly what God intends for all who are reborn in him.*

Essential Influences

When a plant breaks through the earth, four essential components must be present to ensure its continued growth and maturity. The first is the constant nourishment from the soil. The second is light and warmth from the sun. The third is the moisture provided by spring rains and watering. And finally, the fourth key element is carbon dioxide, or CO_2, which the new plants extract from the air. (Carbon dioxide is a subject all its own that reveals another great truth that will be addressed in the next chapter.) This reminds me of how essential the three persons of the Trinity are to our spiritual growth and maturity.

After Jesus rose from the dead, he appeared to his disciples and followers several different times. He wanted to prove to them that he really had been resurrected and he had some final instructions to give before he ascended into heaven. He commissioned them to take both his authority and teaching out into the world and present the kingdom of God. One such event is recorded near the end of the Gospel of Luke. On this occasion, Jesus illuminated the disciples' minds so they could grasp the reality that he was the fulfillment of all Old Testament prophecy concerning the Messiah. He also gave them clear marching orders for their role in spreading the gospel to all the nations in the world. This particular passage is important because it is one of the few places in Scripture where we clearly see the roles of the three persons of the Trinity—the Father, the Son, and the Holy Spirit. Jesus said to them:

> "When *I* [the Son] was with you before, *I* told you that everything written about me in the law of Moses and the prophets and in the Psalms must be fulfilled." Then he opened their minds to understand the Scriptures. And he said, "Yes, it was written long ago that the *Messiah* [the Son of God] would suffer and die and rise from the dead on the third day. It was also written that this message would be proclaimed in the authority of his name to all the nations, beginning in Jerusalem: 'There is forgiveness of sins for all who repent.' You are witnesses of all these things. And now I will send the *Holy Spirit*, just as my *Father* promised. But stay here in the city until the *Holy Spirit* comes and fills you with power from heaven."
>
> Luke 24:44–49 NLT

78

The inner working of the Trinity in the life of the authentic Christian is as important as the soil, sun, and rain are to the seed. Without these three natural essentials all working together, the seed will never reach maturity and will eventually die, just as the believer will die without the inner work of the Father, Son, and Holy Spirit. If Christians are to grow into the fullness of everything God has for us and into the very person he has created us to become, we need more than an intellectual understanding of the Trinity. We need more than a theology concerning the functions and roles of the three personas of God. We need a firsthand revelation of them and a personal experience with them. In the early years of my journey with God, I met the Trinity in unique and amazing ways.

A Revelation of the Father—Creator

It has been my experience that the Christian journey almost always begins with a revelation of the reality of the Father, who is the Creator. I liken this first realization to a seed that receives its start in life when it sinks its roots deep into the richness of the soil. Again in Paul's prayer for the Ephesians, he said, "I pray that . . . your roots will grow down into God's love and keep you strong. And may you have the power to understand, as all God's people should, how wide, how long, how high, and how deep his love is" (Eph. 3:16–18 NLT). Paul desired that the Ephesians receive a revelation of the Father's love.

When this first happened for me, I was sixteen years old. Although I had been raised in the church, I had never made a personal, willful commitment to pursue God. He was the God of my parents and people I respected, but up until an evening on the side of a mountain, I wasn't sure what I truly believed.

My parents gave me a 1956 VW Bug for my sixteenth birthday. Having a vehicle of my own at that age gave me a feeling of independence and freedom that was new and invigorating. That old car was a classic and I thoroughly enjoyed it. In those days the only Volkswagens in America had been shipped directly from Europe, and their speedometers recorded kilometers instead of miles. The back window was the size of a large watermelon, and the signal indicators popped out of the side of the car between the front door and the backseat window. The gas pedal looked like a small wooden donut and there was no fuel gauge—only a lever mounted on the floor that could be flipped over, giving an additional liter of gas when the small tank ran out. Its thirty-horsepower engine could be compared to that of a large lawn mower, but with the help of a brisk tailwind it would go at least 60 kilometers per hour (the equivalent of 45 mph). It was all I needed to expand my horizons.

With my hands on the steering wheel of my own car, the first thing I wanted to do was drive to the old ranch on Liebre Mountain and spend a weekend all by myself. This was the same ranch that Nancy and I later lived on for the first twenty years of our marriage. In those days it was used only as our family's occasional weekend cabin. And so with my parents' blessing, I packed a little food and my sleeping bag, and I took off for what would become one of the most significant and memorable experiences of my teen years.

Alone

To get to the ranch I had to drive up a steep, winding, forty-mile grade that was referred to in those days as the Old Ridge Route. Today it is a modern four-lane freeway known as Interstate 5, which connects Southern California to the San Joaquin Valley. The Ridge Route was a treacherous pull for any vehicle and was well known for taking a mechanical toll on many a car or truck. Driving it alone in my old VW gave me a wonderful sense of adventure.

I arrived at the ranch gate around mid-afternoon, found the key hidden slyly under a rock, and continued up the quarter-mile rocky drive. When I turned off the engine and opened the door, I remember thinking I had never experienced such silence. Always before when we arrived at the cabin, the family was together and there was an excitement and busyness as we unpacked the car. But that day all I felt was the solitude. It was the first time in my sixteen years that I had been all alone, and it felt almost eerie. To shake off my feeling of discomfort, I opened the cabin, built a fire in the fireplace, and heated some water for tea. I drank my tea and cooked an early dinner, not knowing what else to do with myself.

When I finished eating and washing my few dishes, I realized that there were still several hours of daylight left. I wasn't really bored but I felt unsettled being so alone with myself, as though I were slightly off balance and uncertain. In an effort to avoid the onrush of anxiety, I decided to take a hike up Liebre Mountain.

The apostle Paul said in Romans 1: "For ever since the world was created, people have seen the earth and sky. Through everything God made, they can clearly see his invisible qualities—his eternal power and divine nature. So they have no excuse for not knowing God" (v. 20 NLT). Paul was referring to God the Father, the creator of heaven and earth, and I was about to meet him face-to-face.

Before I started my walk, I noticed a small pad of paper and a pencil on my great-grandfather's old secretary desk, which sat in the corner of the cabin. Without much thought, I picked them up and put them into my shirt pocket. With determination I began the steep climb up the forested mountainside. I followed an old game trail that contoured the rugged terrain and went along the upper edge of Robinson Canyon, which had been named after my family years before. The huge white oaks that were so evident lower down disappeared as I climbed higher. In their place stood Coulter pines and massive big cone spruce, and although a smaller species, they resembled the giant Sequoia redwoods. The air was fresh and clear, and the wind in the trees stirred something new in my inner being that I hadn't known before. Though unaware of it at the time, God was setting me up for an encounter with him.

Aware

After about a mile hike upward, I came out into a clearing that provided a vantage point of the entire west end of the Mojave Desert and the Tehachapi Mountains on the vast desert's distant edge. The majestic view stopped me in my tracks and lured me to sit and pause a moment. I sat there for nearly an hour completely captured by not only the view but the smell of the forest and the unbelievable freshness of the mountain air. Everything was so still and quiet around me that I believe my soul became still for the first time—so still that I was able to really listen. I was captivated by the creation and became totally and completely aware of the Creator.

At this point in the story, I have to remind you that I had just turned sixteen and did not feel particularly gifted in writing. English had been the worst of my subjects in high school, mainly because of my extreme dyslexia. But at that moment on the mountain, I was compelled to put into words what I was feeling. I pulled out that small pad of paper and pencil and began to express my emotions as I wrote them out in words.

> And the voices roared, "Too little proof!"
> And I replied, "I have broken from the dense pines
>   and there I have smelled the sap, and felt the earth.
>   I have heard the silence and lifted my head to it.
> And as far as I could see was beauty.
> The swift shadows of clouds on silver fields.
> The colored sunset.
> The jagged Sierras smothered into the endless
>   deserts."
> And now I say, "Have not I seen the face of the
>   Lord?"

I've kept that small piece of paper all these years, a little embarrassed at my first attempt at being poetic. But that short poem, a string of words I put together with much emotion, represented a deep reality that took place in my life that night. For the first time in my sixteen years of life, I had tapped into the reality of God the Father. I knew then that the creation couldn't have been the result of a great accident, and if the creation wasn't an accident, then I wasn't either. It was the first time I had stopped long enough and become still enough to recognize the handprint of God and hear his whisper. And although it was no more than a whisper, I heard it as clearly as if it were spoken directly to my spirit, assuring me I had been uniquely and wonderfully created for a special, even divine, purpose. It would be many years before I discovered that purpose, but it was a beginning. My young, tender root had tapped into and was drawing nourishment from the Father—the good soil—and my journey toward spiritual maturity had begun.

A Revelation of Jesus—the Son

For many reasons the old ranch has always been a special place for me, and that clearing where God first revealed himself to me became a place that I would revisit many times in the years that followed. One such time took place ten years later, after Nancy and I were married and had made the ranch on Liebre Mountain our home. It was during this period of time that we were attending Chapel in the Pines in our local community, and I was wrestling with my new relationship with Jesus. As I shared in a previous chapter, it was a turbulent time between Nancy and me, and although I had publicly confessed faith in Christ, I still didn't really get it. It is one thing to say yes to him in faith, but quite another to know in your "knower," your deepest being, that he really does exist and is not just in heaven but in your everyday life. Being honest with myself, I had to admit I wasn't there yet.

A Thirsty Soul

One night Nancy and I were invited to attend a musical production at a church in Lancaster, California. This was during the late seventies, and the church was one of the more affluent congregations in town, so their multimedia equipment was cutting edge for the day. This was the first time I had witnessed two slide projectors operating in unison with music, as well as in harmony with each other. While the image from one projector faded out, that of the other projector could appear. It was impressive and stirring. As the evening progressed, I noticed a recurring theme from Psalm 42: "As the deer pants for streams of water, so my soul pants for you, O God. My soul thirsts for God, for the living God. When can I go and meet with God?" (vv. 1–2).

I don't remember much of what was said that night, but I do remember that as the choir sang a song based on this psalm, the two slide projectors periodically faded in and out with pictures of a deer. It was the face of a doe that had large brown compassionate eyes. The eyes captured me. When the production ended, the pastor came up and shared the essence of the gospel as only Baptists can. It was a clear message of salvation through Christ, and I remember feeling challenged to commit my life to Christ all over again. When every eye was closed and every head was bowed, I was tempted to raise my hand, knowing that I still needed something I hadn't yet experienced when it came to Jesus. I hesitated and refrained because I believed that to do so would void or cancel out my previous attempt at saying yes to him. I left that night feeling frustrated with myself and very confused.

It was long after dark by the time we got back to the ranch and tucked the kids into bed. I told Nancy I needed to take a walk and be alone for a while. I headed for the clearing with the knoll where I had my first encounter with God as a teenager. It had become a familiar place for me to go at times when I felt unsettled over something. Even in the darkness of night, I easily found my way to it. We had used this spot several times as a place for holding sunrise services for our neighbors at Easter. A few years before, I had erected a cross in the clearing; it was built out of two oak limbs. I had also carved an open Bible out of a large block of wood, which I hung on the front of the cross. With the help of a few friends, I had cut pine logs to serve as benches for folks to sit on during the services. It was there that I sat and prayed earnestly. Somehow that night I prayed in a different way than I had ever prayed before. My prayer was sincere and purposeful; and out of my deep frustration and the confusion I felt, I prayed to God expressing my need and desire to know if Jesus was real and if the things I had heard about him earlier that evening were true. It was more than a prayer; it was a cry from my heart. I really wanted to know.

The Presence of the Lord

I was sitting on a log directly in front of the cross, and although the night was dark, a half moon peeked around passing clouds, periodically illuminating the spring grass and wildflowers that grew around the makeshift altar. I continued to pray for Jesus to reveal himself to me, when all at once I heard footsteps coming out of the thick woods behind me. I must admit that I was seriously terrified. It wasn't so much that I was afraid of wild animals, although there were both bears and mountain lions that lived on the mountain; I was scared because I had just been seriously praying for God to show up, and I was convinced he was right behind me. I sat there frozen, unable to move.

I was actually afraid to turn around and see what was only a few feet away. Whatever or whoever it was took his time, obviously aware but unafraid of me. I sat motionless for what seemed like hours but in reality was only minutes, when a deer stepped over my log bench. She was literally within arm's reach. She walked right in front of the old cross, and then turned around and looked directly into my eyes. I will never forget her eyes because they looked exactly like the eyes that had so captivated me in the pictures I had seen at the church just a few hours before. Then the words of that Psalm rang in my mind again: "As the deer pants for streams of water, so my soul pants for you, O God. My soul thirsts for God, for the living God. When can I go and meet with God?"

That deer never actually spoke to me in words, but she did continue to stare at me as she stood a few feet in front of me. It was both eerie and amazing, but my anxious spirit was calmed and I felt a deep peace. I knew I was in the presence of the Lord and that he had used a deer to reveal himself to me that night. I am certain the event was the orchestration of the Lord. This was his doing, and at that moment I knew the message of the gospel was true—Jesus was real and he cared about me. That night as I watched the deer turn and wander off the knoll, I thanked God for meeting with me and for using his natural creation to speak to me once again. If you asked me when I received Jesus as both my Lord and my Savior, I would have to say I'm not completely sure, but I do know that I never questioned his existence again after that profound evening on the mountain.

A Revelation of the Holy Spirit

This all took place at the beginning of the charismatic renewal of the seventies and eighties. The word *charisma* means "gifts of grace." These gifts are received as a result of the Holy Spirit's indwelling in the life of a Christian believer, bringing to the believer many wonderful benefits. One is the ability to enter into a deeper life with God and thus the ability to become more like Jesus. We call this gift "sanctification" or "holiness." As we allow the Holy Spirit to take charge of our lives, we start to become more Christlike, reflecting his character and attributes through our behaviors and actions. We begin to bear the "fruit of the Holy Spirit" as recorded in Galatians 5.

Gifts of the Spirit

The charismas or gifts were also spoken of throughout the book of Acts and the Epistles as being special abilities to do the whole ministry of Jesus. This encompassed not only the acts of compassion and mercy but the performance of his miracles. Jesus told his disciples concerning the miracles,

> Believe me when I say that I am in the Father and the Father is in me; or at least believe on the evidence of the miracles themselves. I tell you the truth, anyone who has faith in me will do what I have been doing. He will do even greater things than these, because I am going to the Father.
>
> John 14:11–12

And then he explained by adding, "And I will ask the Father, and he will give you another Counselor to be with you forever—the Spirit of truth" (vv. 16–17).

As the charismatic movement swept through both the Protestant and Catholic Church in the late seventies and early eighties, millions of Christians around the world were experiencing the phenomenon of the empowering of the Spirit. Nancy and I were young Christians in those early days, and so much of what we were exposed to was both amazing and confusing. It was undeniable that God was allowing us to experience and witness miracles. We saw miracles in many of the services we attended. Some people were dramatically delivered of demonic influences, others were genuinely healed of physical disabilities, and still others were emotionally set free from things that had paralyzed them mentally. To observe all this as fairly new Christians made it an eye-opening and mind-altering period of time. We were like young plants that had just broken out of the ground into a world of light. We felt free and energized to reach out and up to the inviting warmth and brightness of the sun—and the Son.

We felt as though God was literally transforming us, and we began to crave his presence and the understanding of his divine purpose for our lives. Like the small plants in my garden whose first fragile shoots reached up to the sun's light and warmth, we too were driven to raise our hearts and hands to Jesus, the Son of God, as an act of gratitude and worship. It was an expression of incredible adoration and thanksgiving.

In the heat of the charismatic movement, the book of Acts served as the primary textbook. Everyone was talking about the "baptism of the Spirit," and nearly every service offered opportunities for folks to receive it. Night after night people were being prayed for at the altar or at the front of churches. I can remember watching it all and wondering how much of what was happening was really God and how much was our own wishful thinking. My understanding was that the infilling or baptism of the Spirit was to empower and change human lives so people could go and do what the people did in the book of Acts.

The Holy Spirit relates to people in three different ways, which were characterized by the prepositions *with*, *in*, and *upon*. The Holy Spirit is *with* all people whether they are saved or not. It is the Spirit who woos us to God and shows us our need for him before we even know him. The Spirit is *with* us when he orchestrates events and often uses others to awaken us to his presence. The Spirit is *in* us at the moment we receive Christ. His presence indwells our hearts, ministering to us and enabling the fruit of the Spirit to grow and mature in our lives. The Spirit comes *upon* us when we ask for and receive his empowering for service and ministry. This is also referred to as "receiving the baptism of the Spirit."

The purpose for the gifts of the Spirit, or the charismas, is that God can work through us in the same way as recorded in 1 Corinthians 12. These gifts are described as words of wisdom, words of knowledge, the special gift of faith, healing, miracles, prophecy, the distinguishing of spirits, the gift of tongues, and the interpretation of tongues (vv. 8–10). All of these special gifts are given to us so we can effectively present and demonstrate the kingdom of God to a world that has yet to know him.

A Mighty, Rushing Wind

The teaching on the Holy Spirit that we received was based on solid biblical truth, and many who heard it pursued the empowering of the Spirit for pure and right reasons. It was an amazing and impacting time because God continually showed up in our meetings and demonstrated his presence.

However, there were those who misunderstood the purpose of the infilling of the Spirit, seeing it as merely a means to a greater personal encounter with God; some simply craved the experience. They somehow did not understand that having the Spirit *in* your heart was all anyone needed to fully encounter and experience the presence of God's love. Because of this misunderstanding, some people looked continually for personal manifestations of the Spirit, going time and again to the altar to be empowered or touched by him. Failing to understand that the empowering was for ministry, many never took the Holy Spirit's gift to the streets to minister to the world at large. Everyone was excited about what God was doing, but in many cases few lives were being changed.

Seeing both the amazing acts of God and the self-centered motives of people, I became confused as I attempted to sort out what was authentic and what was man-made. A major turning point in my journey with God took place on a night when all this was going through my head. We were at a typical charismatic service at our church in Lancaster. There was a ministry time going on, and many were going forward to receive the baptism of the Spirit. I was skeptical and resistant, but at the same time I was hungry for all that God had for me. I was in turmoil and there was a battle going on in my spirit. Finally I decided to die to myself and go forward for prayer as I desperately wanted more of God. While I stood there receiving the prayers of others, I felt nothing. As they prayed more fervently, I became convinced that I might never experience more; in my mind I decided that nothing was going to happen. I knew that Nancy had already experienced a wonderful encounter with the Spirit, and I had seen very real changes in her life because of it. As for me—I figured I was too unemotional and analytical for such a thing to happen to me. When the ministry time was over, we headed back to the old ranch. Feeling a bit discouraged, I decided I needed to take a walk on the mountain once again.

It was a perfectly still and beautiful summer evening. All the stars were out when I ventured up toward the old cross on my now very familiar knoll. I had only gotten about a hundred yards from the cabin when for some reason I decided to change my destination. Instead of making the long hike up the mountain, I decided to sit on a fence that bordered our orchard. I sat on the top rail facing the canyon that cut deep into the mountain rising before me. As I sat there in the stillness of the night, I began to pray another one of those heartfelt, honest prayers. I said, "God, I need to know about this Holy Spirit thing. If this is really you and you want it for me, then I want it. Amen." That was it in a nutshell, short but sweet. I wanted everything God had for me, but I had to know that it was really *from him* and that it was his will that I receive it. And that's when it happened.

I continued to sit in the still, dark quiet, and I began to hear the wind coming faintly. It was not around me or even near me but rather high up on the mountain above me. It was quiet at first but grew in intensity as it slowly moved down the deep canyon before me. It was not normal and, like my experience with the deer, I was frightened. At that moment all I could remember was the teaching from earlier that evening; it had been about the mighty, rushing wind in Acts 2 that came into the upper room and changed the apostles' lives forever. I was convinced that God was coming down the mountain and he was coming for me.

The wind got closer and closer, and yet it was nowhere around me. It sounded like a freight train roaring down the canyon, and moments before it

I wanted everything God had for me, but I had to know that it was really from him and that it was his will that I receive it.

got to me, I gripped the rail I was sitting on and braced myself for impact. It hit me head-on and as it did, shivers went up my spine and the hair stood up on the back of my neck. I started to cry for no reason other than the simple fact that I had felt the full impact of God's presence *with*, *in*, and *upon* me. And then the wind was gone. I mean gone—in a split second it was nowhere to be seen or heard. I sat there again in absolute silence, but now filled with wonder and awe. I knew that what I had just experienced was real; and if it was real, I knew I was somehow being called into God's service. Unbeknownst to me then, this would lead to a life of full-time ministry.

6

Photosynthesis

Transformed to Serve

Nancy and I have always felt a magnetic pull to the solitude and freshness of the country. This pull is unseen yet very real and very powerful. Although I haven't fully understood it, I do know I feel a certain freedom there as well as the ability to think more clearly. Whenever I spend time in places where the air is fresh, my creative juices flow with new ideas. Somehow I have more faith and courage to believe and move on impossible dreams, trusting in God for guidance. I know the absence of distraction has a lot to do with it; but more than that, I think the human mind and thus the spirit both crave and thrive in the presence of pure, unobstructed, oxygenated air.

After living the first twenty years of our marriage on the old family homestead, Nancy and I moved our family to Boise, Idaho, a thriving city with a growing population of nearly two hundred thousand. Our move was predicated on the dream and vision of starting a new church. It was an exciting and necessary season of our life, but life in Boise was very different for us. For the first time, we were within walking distance of a major supermarket and several restaurants and convenience stores. Our son, Brook, could walk or ride his bike to school, and our daughter, Kate, who had just turned sixteen, could drive herself around town.

There were advantages to city life, for sure, but for the first time we became aware of gray noise that could be heard twenty-four hours a day—traffic passing on a major thoroughfare two blocks away, lawn mowers and other machines, as well as our neighbors' indiscernible conversations. We had always slept at night with our windows open, letting the cool evening air recharge our home with freshness for the coming day, but we soon realized our habits had to adapt to this new lifestyle. We recognized the advantage of an air-conditioning system that would allow us to keep our windows closed for security reasons and filter the invading new sounds and smells that interrupted the solitude we had been accustomed to for so long.

It was necessary to live close to the new church when it was first planted. In the beginning I was the only pastor, and I was on call 24-7. I did all the weddings, all the funerals, all the hospital calls day and night, and needed to be ready and available at any given moment. We had all of the new church's leadership training in our living room, and even the youth group used our home as a meeting place. There was no getting around it—we needed to be city folks at least for a while, and for that season we adapted to the new lifestyle, actually relishing the adventure of city living, which lasted for nine years.

By the late nineties, the church had developed and matured to a point of becoming less dependent on Nancy's and my constant attention. We had built the first of our campus facilities on a twenty-two-acre property in the city. By that time we also had a very gifted staff, which included other pastors and support personnel. Finally we were entering a new season in which we were no longer needed at every meeting or responsible for every pastoral call.

By this time our kids had gone on to college, and Nancy and I began to feel a bit liberated from the responsibilities that had motivated us to live in the heart of the city. In addition, my parents, who had been living on the old ranch in California, had decided to move to Boise too. This meant we were able to sell our portion of the original family ranch. With that sale, Nancy and I had the resources to leave the city once again and return to the fresh air of the open countryside.

While living in Boise, we had bought and sold several homes, pouring into them hours of sweat equity and hard work in improvements. Each place was remodeled and transformed; in fact we had moved three different times during this period of city living. In the end we reached our goal to return to our old country lifestyle and became established on our homestead at the base of Timber Butte, about an hour from Boise.

A Miraculous Conversion

In Romans 1 Paul said man is without excuse when it comes to knowing God, because God has revealed himself through his creation. Paul wrote, "For since the creation of the world God's invisible qualities—his eternal power and divine nature—have been clearly seen, being understood from what has been made, so that men are without excuse" (v. 20).

I have come to realize that air, being invisible, is a very powerful picture of one of God's greatest invisible qualities—his desire and miraculous ability to transform the human heart and life.

Have you ever wondered why being in the great outdoors is so invigorating, especially in dense forests or open meadows or the beaches of a vast ocean shoreline? In places like these, there is an invisible quality of oxygen that is free from pollution and rich in abundance. Oxygen is a miraculous substance that is life-giving, and its purity literally determines the quality of every living thing on earth, which includes your life and mine. Like God, oxygen is invisible and is often forgotten and taken for granted. And like God, oxygen must be present every minute of every day for life to be sustained on the planet. It is a gift and a miracle, which takes us to the next stage of our parable of the good soil.

God planted the seed in the good soil so that it could take root and grow to maturity. Already we have discovered that God allows and uses brokenness and seasons of isolation for the seed's root to penetrate into the richness of his soil. We have compared our own growth as spiritual beings to the life of the seed that sinks its roots into the nourishment of his love and provision until we finally break out of the comfort and security of the soil into the open air. This is a whole new phase of development for both the young fragile plant and for us. As the plant spreads its first tiny stems and leaves, it receives energy from the light of the sun, absorbs water from the rains, and for the first time begins to convert these provisions from God into life-giving oxygen. This is the beginning of a perfect picture of God working through the life of a young Christian who is now ready to use God's provision for the sake of others. In the plant world, this process is called photosynthesis; for us it is spiritual transformation.

For twelve years I was a junior high school teacher and taught biology for many of those years. I learned how some of the most fascinating, wonderful, and miraculous things nature has to offer can come across as both boring and monotonous if not communicated with passion and simplicity. As we cover the topic of photosynthesis, I sense the danger of possible boredom. At the same time I desperately want my students to understand this crucial and miraculous concept in the life of plants.

The same is true as we think of photosynthesis in spiritual terms, so bear with me.

Photosynthesis is nothing short of a miracle, and without it nothing on our planet would be able to live. It is a phenomenon of transformation that takes place primarily in the leaves of plants growing on dry land and within the ocean. Plants use the energy from sunlight to produce sugar (which becomes the fuel that nourishes all living things) and convert carbon dioxide (a gas that poisons all air-breathing life) with the aid of water into life-giving oxygen.

A leaf may be viewed as a solar collector constructed of thousands of photosynthetic cells, which are used to make this amazing conversion that literally turns death to life. The leaf is able to do this because it contains the green pigment called chlorophyll, an extremely complex molecule that isn't fully understood. This miraculous conversion process is completely and totally dependent on chlorophyll. It not only absorbs the rays of the sun but also sorts them out and reflects them. When a pigment sorts a certain light ray, it reflects its color; in the case of chlorophyll it is green. Therefore oxygen-emitting plants are seen in various shades of green. If you were to use a chemical equation, it would translate as follows: six molecules of water + six molecules of carbon dioxide = one molecule of sugar + six molecules of oxygen.

To summarize and keep it simple, let me list the main points we need to understand concerning photosynthesis:

1. Photosynthesis uses certain rays of sunlight to energize the conversion of carbon dioxide and water into sugar and oxygen.
2. Photosynthesis gives off life-giving air and captures and stores carbon (a substance that can destroy life that requires oxygen).
3. Photosynthesis creates oxygen and extracts nutrients and water from the soil, producing a sugar substance that provides nutrition to animals that eat and digest foliage.

Simply stated, photosynthesis is a miraculous process by which substances that would become death-causing poisons are turned into substances that nourish and produce life.

Our Purpose in the Kingdom

In Ecclesiastes 3:11 King Solomon wrote that God has put eternity in the hearts of men. In other words, God has programmed us to discover the reality of his existence as well as our purpose in his kingdom. Remembering this when we read Paul's words in Romans 12 sheds new light on this passage of Scripture: "Don't copy the behavior and customs of this world, but let God transform you into a new person by changing the way you think. Then you will learn to know God's will for you" (v. 2 NLT). We are to be transformed so that God can use us to help transform others from a state of spiritual death to new life.

> *God has programmed us to discover the reality of his existence as well as our purpose in his kingdom.*

Paul also told us earlier in the book of Romans: "The wages of sin is death, but the free gift of God is eternal life in Christ Jesus our Lord" (6:23 NASB). This death Paul speaks of is the death that the human spirit is destined to experience outside of a relationship with Christ; it is the death that Jesus came to reverse for anyone who would receive his provision of life. Not everyone will, but for those who do, everything begins to change.

The change that transpires as a result of entering into a new life with God has a ripple effect that begins to transform the heart. The hardened heart that once plagued us softens; our heart becomes merciful and compassionate instead of harsh and judgmental. The ripple continues on, transforming and renewing the mind, and we begin to view the world differently than we have ever seen it before. Literally we recycle our old worldview for a kingdom view; we now begin to see things from a Christlike perspective. What we used to think was okay may not seem so any longer. The sin that once caused us to move toward spiritual and emotional death is viewed differently as our newly transformed thinking process moves us toward acts of righteousness.

The ripple moves ever outward as it transforms our behavior and actions. We begin to treat others differently, caring about and taking into consideration their feelings and life circumstances. As a result, we become better neighbors, friends, co-workers, parents, and spouses. Like the chlorophyll in the plant's leaf that reflects the green rays of the sun's light, we begin to reflect the light or truth of the Son.

At this point our transformation can be seen for the first time. In this transforming process, we are becoming more Christlike, not only in our theology but in our behavior and life actions. The ripple goes on and on until we eventually capture God's heart for a broken world and are motivated to do something about it.

Spiritual Photosynthesis

I distinctly remember a moment in 1982 when this transformation process took place in me and changed my values and perception about what was really important, which consequently redirected my life motives. I wasn't expecting it or looking for it; it just happened. And when it did, I realized immediately that Nancy's and my life had just stepped into an unknown abyss of adventure and uncertainty.

After my trip with Brother Andrew's ministry, Open Doors Asia, when I smuggled Bibles into China, I had become ruined for any kind of normal life; I had become discontent with what I perceived as a lifestyle that was somewhat status quo. During my trip to China, I had been exposed to a world I didn't know existed, and I desperately wanted to experience more of it. A new hunger was awakened and began to stir within me. I felt a need to use my life more effectively, and I wasn't quite sure what to do about it. At that time one of our contacts with Open Doors Asia was a man named Sony Lagardo. He was based in Bangkok, Thailand, and had been courageously connecting with underground and persecuted Christian people groups in Vietnam, Laos, and Burma.

One such group was the Karen Hill Tribe people who were undergoing ethnic cleansing under the oppression of the Communist Burmese. An estimated one million Karen had taken refuge along the Burma-Thailand border, forming an army of their own to protect their families. They had been fighting for their independence since 1948. Many of the Karen tribes had become Christians in the early 1800s as a result of the courageous efforts of Adoniram Judson. Judson was the first foreign American missionary and had dedicated his entire adult life to the hill tribes of Burma.

My pastor, Brent Rue, had a growing passion to serve Open Doors Asia through our church. Sony asked Brent to send a small team into a specific Karen village. The village was the military and civil headquarters of this new unofficial Karen nation known then as Kathellee. The purpose of the trip was to see how the outside church might be able to serve the Karen in their survival efforts. I was asked to go on this fact-finding mission along with two other men. Because of what the Lord had been doing in me, I was ready and willing.

After flying to Thailand and connecting with Sony, we took a bus eight hours north to the border town of Mae

Sot. (Years later Mae Sot would become the home of thousands of Karen refugees who would be confined there in large camps.) Here we met our first Karen contacts who loaded us into a small four-wheel-drive pickup and drove us another five hours north through the canopied jungle. All along the way, we encountered check stations guarded with armed Thai soldiers who stopped and aggressively questioned our intentions, waving their guns in our faces. Periodically the Karen men escorting us paid bribes, until we finally arrived at a ramp on the bank of the Moei River and boarded a colorful, long, narrow Karen boat.

For three or four hours we traveled down the river, at times navigating around rocks and log snags and through stretches of rapids. Along the shores we observed secluded machine gun nests and small villages where Karen men carried M16 rifles as if they were natural extremities of their bodies. We were later told their weapons had been procured on the black market from the leftover stockpiles of the Vietnam War. I felt vulnerable, off balance, and completely at the mercy of a people whose language and customs I could not understand.

We arrived at the headquarters village that would be our home for the next two weeks. After being escorted up the river's rock ledge and past dozens of stilted bamboo huts, we were introduced to our host, a man named Saw Shwe Ya Hai, who was draped in the traditional colorful garb of his village. He was also the head of education for the developing Karen nation, full of passion and determination to accomplish his agenda.

To our delight and relief, we found that Shwe Ya Hai spoke English. His wife, Capri, served us tea, and after some polite and casual small talk, he told us what he needed. He said that the Karen people were desperate to learn English because it was an absolute necessity for their survival. He said that without it they couldn't connect with the outside world and convince other nations of their dire situation. It was his job to provide English classes in every village along the river.

Knowing in advance that we were coming and that I had a degree in secondary education, Shwe Ya Hai had gathered twenty or thirty of his teachers. Many traveled several days to come and sit under my instruction. He wanted to make every minute count, so that very afternoon I began working with the Karen teachers. For two weeks I worked from morning until night teaching conversational English to a group of people who had never spoken it before.

Never in my life had I experienced students so hungry for information. They were not only motivated but extremely intelligent and learned very fast. Long before I arrived, they had been reading English in an attempt to learn it on their own—but they had little experience at either hearing or speaking it themselves. They were timid the first few days but soon became comfortable as any intimidation on either side began to melt away. In time we started to relax, and after only a week and a half I realized we were actually able to communicate enough to talk about things of importance. I was becoming very attached to my new students, and one afternoon toward the end of my visit, I found myself wanting to tell them about the love of God.

That night I stayed up late digging through my Bible. The idea of communicating any biblical truth was all new to me, and I felt completely inadequate to do it, but God had put a supernatural love in my heart for these new friends and I desperately wanted to tell them about it. Not knowing where else to begin, I looked up every reference concerning love in the New Testament. I worked until very late, long after the gaslights had been put out. I resorted to using my flashlight until the batteries began to fade. Finally giving up, I prayed and fell asleep after asking the Holy Spirit for help.

> *I was experiencing "spiritual photosynthesis" for the first time in my Christian life.*

The next morning I preached the first Bible message of my life. It was clumsy and basic but heartfelt, and I knew they understood. The tears that filled the eyes of my students revealed that they comprehended what I was saying and that God was supernaturally using me to provide life-giving truth to them. I was experiencing "spiritual photosynthesis" for the first time in my Christian life. God was connecting the truth of the Son, the love of the Father, and the empowering of the Spirit and conveying this treasure from my life into theirs. No longer was my faith journey just about me; now it was God working through me. Like a plant that gives off life-giving oxygen, I was being used to convert God's truth and power into a meaningful message. It was wonderful and exhilarating, and I knew then that it was what I wanted to do with the rest of my life.

Responding to God's Call

Later, as I stood in the Moei River on the border of Burma and Thailand taking a bath, it all came together.

I'd been smitten by the love of God. He had exposed me to a new kind of love, not a human love but an agape love, his love, for a broken world that desperately needed to know him. I had fallen in love with a people I'd known for only two weeks, and my heart was full and broken all at the same time.

The Karen people were destitute and desperate. They were a people without a country and without significant allies. Nearly every person I met had experienced horrible atrocities that I had no concept of or ability to truly comprehend. My limited worldview couldn't grasp the concept of ethnic cleansing, and it broke me. These precious new friends had lost family members or close relations who had been killed by the Burmese in an effort to rid the world of them. I simply didn't understand how this could be happening. And in the midst of such horrific conditions, the Thai government tolerated the Karen settling along their border but refused to let them immigrate into their society. It seemed no one wanted them, and few even knew of their plight. Something had to be done. I realized God was calling me to play some small part in relieving their struggles, though I had no idea what that would be.

As our flight back to the States headed for the Los Angeles International Airport, Nancy prepared to come and meet me at the airport. She had planned to come with the wives of the others on the team but sensed a prompting of the Lord to drive our car alone instead. Somehow she knew our lives were about to change, and although she was a bit fearful of what could happen, she knew God had called her to say yes to whatever it was. Years before she had prayed I would become a man who would weep before the Lord and become the spiritual leader of our home. For Nancy, trusting me now was a simple but scary act of obedience.

I remember how excited I was to see Nancy and to be back on American soil after such a precarious and emotionally stretching trip. As we exited the plane that afternoon and reunited with our families, there was excitement, laughter, and rapid-fire storytelling of our short but amazing adventure. I'll never forget leaving my traveling companions and finally getting into the car alone with Nancy. We paid our parking ticket and got on the freeway heading north toward the ranch. As Nancy drove, she asked me how I was doing. I opened my mouth with every intention of telling her what had transpired and how God had been changing my heart for the world, when I began to sob uncontrollably. I cried for what seemed like an hour of our two-hour drive home. When I finally gained enough control, I told Nancy that I believed God was calling us as a family back to the Karen people.

More to Do

Nine months later I resigned my position as a schoolteacher, packed up our young family, and headed back to Thailand. Initially it was our intention to become full-time workers in the Karen villages, but because of the aggressive war efforts of the Burmese in the 1980s, it was impossible to stay among them permanently. On our first trip back, we were working in a camp on the Burmese side of the border. We were there on a two-month teaching assignment in which Shwe Ya Hai had once again gathered all the teachers who were able to get to our location.

Unfortunately, during the first week we were awakened in the night and evacuated back across the river into Thailand due to the threat of Burmese mortar fire. We stayed in Mai Sot for three days before we could return and carry on our work. We arrived back in the village on a Sunday, and the Karen were having a baptism in the river after their morning service. When our daughter, Kate, who was nine years old at the time, heard this, she asked if she could be baptized along with the other Karen. I'll never forget how the riverbank was lined with Karen soldiers armed to the hilt with bandoleers of machine gun shells slung over their shoulders as they watched their pastor baptize a young American girl. Over the next few years, we returned seven different times to work with the Karen, moving up and down the Moei and Salween rivers, building deep relationships with a people we learned to love.

It was during this season of our lives that I joined the Vineyard Church staff in Lancaster and served as a missions and education director for eight years. Had it not been for the Karen people, most likely I would never have left my profession in public education and launched out on a new life of full-time ministry. My role on staff gradually changed from an assistant pastor to an associate pastor under Brent's leadership, until 1988 when Nancy and I felt called to plant the new church in Boise, Idaho.

Through the years, we have sent many teams on behalf of the Boise Vineyard into the Karen camps, serving under Shwe Ya Hai, but Nancy and I have never had the opportunity to go back. Even our son, Brook, led a team and was able to reunite with the boys he had played with so many years before, finding that many had become soldiers in the revolution.

Working with the Karen was life changing for our family, and it provided a powerful enhancement to our ministry training that enabled us to build a church with global vision. Somehow, though, I always believed God had an even greater purpose in our love for the Karen. Twenty-five years after our trips into the hill-tribe villages, our next chapter with the Karen unfolded.

It was on a Sunday in the fall of 2007. I had just dismissed the second morning service and walked out of the sanctuary into our front entry hall, a large room we call Heritage Hall where there are bistro-style tables and chairs, with a coffee bar and bookstore on opposite sides. It is a warm and inviting room with a giant hearth and fireplace at one end and actually serves as a family room to our church family.

On this Sunday the room was full of activity—people visiting, laughing, and just hanging out. Parents were reuniting with their children as they filtered out of the children and youth ministry areas. Everything seemed normal until I noticed a group of Asian people of various ages standing in a group on the far side of the room. They caught my attention immediately because they were dressed in distinctly native Karen clothing.

I couldn't believe what I was seeing and excitedly pushed through the crowded room toward them. I introduced myself, but none of them seemed to understand what I was saying until one older gentleman stepped forward and greeted me in broken English. Through a short conversation with him, and then later with refugee relocation workers, I discovered they were the first wave of Karen refugees who were being allowed to relocate in the United States. Amazingly enough, Boise was one of few locations chosen for relocation of the refugees; and by some miracle they had chosen the Boise Vineyard as one of the churches to attend. Our church has a three-acre organic community garden that provides vegetables for people in need, and the Karen had been drawn to it. That morning I knew God had more for us to do with the Karen; his good, pleasing, and perfect will had yet another chapter to be written.

Today the Karen people hold their own services in our facility every Sunday morning. We all meet for worship and praise together at the beginning of the service, and then they leave for a service in their own language. After church, a team of volunteers joins with the Karen in small groups to work on teaching them conversational English. Others look out for their personal needs by helping with resources, shopping, medical visits, and transportation.

Because of our renewed connection with the Karen, we have sent one young woman as a full-time worker into their refugee camps in Thailand, as well as others who have gone on short-term mission trips. God has renewed, enhanced, and accelerated a work that was started years before—seemingly by happenstance but actually with a greater plan than just prompting me into ministry. He has drawn many, many others as well into the service of these precious people in need.

7

Symbiotic Relationships

Becoming Part of an Authentic Community

For nearly forty years Nancy and I have planted a seasonal vegetable garden each spring. After becoming established on our new homestead at the base of Timber Butte, we decided to take this traditional venture to new levels of organic purity and productivity. This meant we chose not to rely on synthetic pesticides, fungicides, herbicides, or chemical fertilizers. We wanted to get away from genetically modified fruits and vegetables so that not only would the food we grew be healthier for us, but the method of production would be safer for the environment. We had started an environmental stewardship ministry in the church a few years before, even publishing two books on the subject. So it was essential for us to practice what I'd been preaching, especially in our personal lives.

A Feeling of Belonging

Some ministries emerged out of our efforts to be an environmentally friendly fellowship, including an organic community garden developed on the church property. This ministry, affectionately known as Garden O' Feedin', has gained national recognition and has expanded over three acres of land. It produces more than twenty-five thousand pounds of produce each season, which is used to feed the poor in our community. The joy and life it has generated attract more than a hundred hardworking volunteers, some of whom have obtained Master Gardener certification from a University of Idaho extension program.

Twice a week our garden volunteers host an open farmers' market for folks who come to get food from the food pantry warehouse. When the ministry first started, it was the only food bank around that provided fresh organic produce in addition to the normal canned and packaged foods that most pantry programs distribute. Today many other churches are following this example, seeing the many benefits a garden can bring to the life of a church community. It generates free, healthy food for people who need it and, equally important, it provides the opportunity for folks to enter into a rich, functional, working community. It has given many, many people a sense of purpose and a feeling of belonging. Somehow, as people have served in the garden, it has brought deeper meaning into their Christian walk. The garden has drawn them into community and given them a skill and expertise that benefit many others. Classes are held for anyone who desires the tools and knowledge of organic vegetable production. Although Nancy and I never managed to attend the classes themselves, we constantly gleaned from the expertise of these amazing gardeners.

The point person and visionary behind Garden O' Feedin' is Bill Meeker. Bill has a wealth of information, and though semiretired, he works as hard as anyone I know, completely dedicating his golden years to running this amazing project. He is a gift to a lot of folks, but for Nancy and me he has been an incredible resource.

Often, especially in the spring, I find myself getting antsy as I sit in the confines of my church office. That's when I feel compelled to go visit Bill. On most days of the week, he is usually found working alongside his volunteers in the garden. My brief visits with him have been invaluable to my success as a vegetable gardener. I've learned about the benefits of raised beds, efficient drip systems, composting, and natural fertilizers. I've also learned about the many advantages of organic gardening and why the food that is produced has so much more nutritional value than non-organic food. I have gained a new respect for the small farmer and realize how commercial synthetic farming operations can be detrimental to the long-term welfare of a world that must be fed to survive. I've come to understand that for organic methods of food production to work, the garden itself must become a symbiotic community.

Living Relationships

The word *symbiotic* refers to the mutual relationships between living species, such as plants, insects, animals, and even microorganisms, where one benefits because of the presence of the others. A symbiotic community is a community that works best when both similar and diverse species are interacting and working together. For example, in an orchard of fruit trees it is essential to have at least two of every fruit species side-by-side so the honeybees and other pollinators (including the wind) will cross-pollinate them. One cherry tree standing alone cannot bear fruit. A community of trees is required—an orchard. Essentially an orchard is a community of trees established for the purpose of bearing fruit. For every tree to fulfill its purpose adequately, a vast variety of organisms must be present, all working together for mutual benefit. This includes even the smallest microorganisms that are at work providing nourishment to root systems.

Another example of this concept of community is on display in every cornfield. Corn must be grown in rows side-by-side if it is to mature and produce ripened ears. One row standing alone, without the protection of the greater crop, will be vulnerable to windstorms. Also, pollination would be hindered. When the wind broadcasts pollen, there must be other rows of corn to receive it. Plants thrive best in symbiotic communities, and so do we.

Compatible, interacting relationships are essential in the plant world, and they are equally important to the church community that hopes to sustain the health and growth of the body. For such a symbiotic community to flourish, five elements of compatible, interacting relationships must be present and working. The five required elements are:

1. the camaraderie of like kinds
2. diversity
3. cooperative participation

4. corporate protection against adversity

5. sustainable regeneration

The Camaraderie of Like Kinds

After the day of Pentecost in the second chapter of Acts, thousands of Christians were brought together with one belief system, united around one cause. Once they had been a people surviving in a confusing and changing culture that had pulled them apart, but their common faith and a new sense of divine purpose drew them into meaningful community. Scripture describes repeatedly the unity and oneness they experienced: "These all with one mind were continually devoting themselves to prayer" (Acts 1:14 NASB); "and all those who had believed were together and had all things in common" (2:44 NASB); "day by day continuing with one mind in the temple, and breaking bread from house to house, they were taking their meals together with gladness and sincerity of heart" (v. 46 NASB); "and the congregation of those who believed were of one heart and soul; and not one of them claimed that anything belonging to him was his own, but all things were common property to them" (4:32 NASB).

Believers throughout the centuries have looked at these first members of the church and esteemed them as the model of a true community of Christian faith because of the tight-knit, interdependent lifestyle they experienced. In the late sixties and early seventies, during what was known as the Jesus Movement, many young Christian converts moved into communes all along the California coastline trying to emulate true biblical community. Few of these communes lasted more than a couple of years before they unraveled and disbanded. It was not because "holding all things in common" was a bad idea, but because a true symbiotic community requires all five elements of interacting relationships. Nancy and I experienced this truth in our early ministry years.

Near the end of my teaching career, Nancy and I received a vision to begin a discipleship school in conjunction with our church in Lancaster, California. We were to do this school on our original family ranch, which by then was owned by someone else. Through a sequence of supernatural circumstances and events, and with the blessing of our pastor Brent Rue, we miraculously secured a long-term lease from the ranch owners to use their property and facilities simply by agreeing to maintain it. No one could believe it, but because God blessed it, it happened. For the next fifteen years, hundreds of young people from all over the world came to the ranch to participate in six-month sessions of intense discipleship under our church's leadership.

I think because of the influence of the communal life models of the Jesus Movement, numbers of discipleship schools sprang up around the world that were disconnected and even isolated from local churches. Organizations like YWAM (Youth With A Mission) and Last Days Ministries were highly popular because they were meeting a discipleship need that most churches weren't adequately providing. Discipleship was being outsourced to specialized parachurch groups like these, and we decided to do the same—though our school was connected to the Lancaster Vineyard rather than being run independently.

Maintaining the ranch and the school was one of our first jobs after I resigned from public education to enter a life of full-time Christian service. The ranch, known then as the

Vineyard Ranch, was an hour from Lancaster. Each school session had about a dozen students who lived together in the solitude and isolation of the mountains. Although Nancy and I lived on our smaller ranch a mile up the road, our days and evenings were spent being fully engaged with our students next door. For the first time in our lives, we experienced living in community where everyone shared everything, including their lives. We worshiped together every morning, had devotions together, ate together, did work details together, shopped together, and cooked together. We also sat together under hours of teaching by pastors and leaders from all over the country who would join our community for a week at a time to teach the students. We shared every part of our lives together, and as a result, we all became like open books. In the process of opening up, the students dealt with past hurts and hidden sin that had paralyzed them emotionally and spiritually. Because of the safety of a controlled environment, the opportunity for open confession and the depth of personal ministry provided deep healing and new freedom.

> *The opportunity for open confession and the depth of personal ministry provided deep healing and new freedom.*

There were aspects of those days that were wonderful, but because our community wasn't completely symbiotic, many students got stuck in their inward self-focus and missed learning about essential aspects of the Christian life, and this later hindered their growth and maturity. While being removed from the greater body of the church, many did not understand the value or purpose of the church. They did not have the training to assimilate back into the normal life of the church, where they could be a functional part of the body.

Although each term of the ranch school provided a season of wonderful ministry experience, it had a tendency to cause our participants to become inward rather than outward focused. Outward focus is necessary if the body of Christ is to have an impact on the broken world we are called to reach. Without the fullness of symbiotic community (all five elements), the discipleship process can become anemic and limited in its ability to grow Christians ready to participate in a harvest of thirty, sixty, and a hundredfold. So we must not overlook the other essential elements of symbiotic community.

Diversity

Not only were these first believers united, but at the same time they were a people of great diversity, and each played a different role and unique part within the greater community. In the book of Acts we read about a married couple named Aquila and Priscilla who were comrades of the apostle Paul. They came in contact with Apollos, a wonderful Bible teacher, who was instructing the people of Ephesus about the Messiah, without knowing the complete story of Jesus. He had been sharing the story up to the point of John the Baptist and how John had announced the coming of the Messiah. Hearing this, Aquila and Priscilla told him the rest of the story.

Apollos became a powerful discipler, while Paul was a powerful evangelist and church planter. They were united as one in their belief concerning Jesus but very diverse in their individual roles. Scripture tells us that people in Corinth started debating among themselves which one of these two men was the better teacher and thus which one they would follow—Apollos or Paul. It was then that Paul wrote, "What then is Apollos? And what is Paul? Servants through whom you believed, even as the Lord gave opportunity to each one. I planted, Apollos watered, but God was causing the growth. So then neither the one who plants nor the one who waters is anything, but God who causes the growth" (1 Cor. 3:5–7 NASB). Again, using the metaphor of the garden, Paul tells us that although we all have different gifts, talents, and responsibilities, only God creates life and makes our growth possible. This is a common problem in many Christian circles when there is no allowance for or the encouragement of diversity in gifting or methodologies when it comes to reaching a wide range of people with the gospel.

In Romans 12, referencing this diversity of gifting that must be present in an authentic community, Paul likens our roles to uniquely different parts of the same body:

> Just as each of us has one body with many members, and these members do not all have the same function, so in Christ we who are many form one body, and each member belongs to all the others. We have different gifts, according to the grace given us. If a man's gift is prophesying, let him use it in proportion to his faith. If it is serving, let him serve; if it is teaching, let him teach; if it is encouraging, let him encourage; if it is contributing to the needs of others, let him give generously; if it is leadership, let him govern diligently; if it is showing mercy, let him do it cheerfully.
>
> Romans 12:4–8

In other words, God created each of us different on purpose, intending for us to bring our uniqueness into the community for the common good. In this way our communities will become more symbiotic in nature and, because of this, more functional.

Cooperative Participation

A symbiotic community thrives best when there is active cooperation and participation among its members. The book of Acts refers to the community as the "fellowship of believers." The Greek word here translated "fellowship" is *koinonia*, which denotes contribution or participation. *Koinonia* is more than simple relationship; it is relationship with a purpose that requires action on the part of its members. Symbiotic community, which is what we are meant to be, requires us to be more than passive members. A fellowship is a community with a purpose, not just a group of people seeking relationship for relationship's sake. When a community loses its sense of purpose, it generally becomes ingrown over time and collapses.

> *God created each of us different on purpose, intending for us to bring our uniqueness into the community for the common good.*

My dad was a torpedo bomber pilot during WWII. He and other members of his squadron flew huge TBM Avengers off the decks of aircraft carriers in the South Pacific. Many of his closest friends lost their lives during some of those vital missions. My dad and his crew actually crashed when his single 1900-horsepower engine failed on a carrier landing approach. Dad was the sole survivor of the crash, losing his entire crew that fateful day. That tragic event had a dramatic, lifelong impact on him.

In 1995 Dad's squadron decided to get together for their fiftieth reunion at a lodge in Fairbanks, Alaska. I'm not sure why they chose a place so far away from where everyone lived, but the date was set and my parents were excited to attend. They hadn't seen any of their old friends and comrades since the end of the war so many years ago. My dad really looked forward to spending quality time with the others from the squadron.

> *A symbiotic community thrives best when there is active cooperation and participation among its members.*

When my parents returned home, I asked about their time with his old friends. I'll never forget my dad's response. He told me how amazing and wonderful it was to see everyone again after all those years. He said it was as if time had stood still. Everyone was much older, but they were still exactly the same as he remembered. Dad shared about the visit they had with everyone, staying for days at the lodge, just reminiscing and telling stories as if they had just happened yesterday. He said they laughed and they cried, and their relationships picked up exactly where they had left off fifty years before.

My father's account of the reunion made me wonder— how is it that people could remain in such deep relationship after being apart for so many years? What was it that could create such a lasting community of men and women? And then it struck me. They had been a community built around a cause much bigger than any one of them. This community had been built not around relationship for relationship's sake, but around a cause, a mighty effort to preserve freedom. They had fulfilled a call as warriors in a great army.

Then reality hit home: Christians too have been called to be an army—the army of God. We too have been called to a great war between good and evil, against powers and principalities of darkness. We too have been called to be ambassadors and warriors in the kingdom of God. With this understanding, I realized that the fellowship of believers in the first-century church was much like that experienced by the men in my dad's squadron; they were people who had to face great adversity for the cause of Christ, a cause worthy of giving one's life.

True *koinonia* requires a symbiotic community in which everyone has a part to play and everyone finds his or her place to participate according to each one's gifts and passions. When that takes place, people begin to feel valued and have a sense of belonging; deep friendships emerge and lasting, meaningful relationships are built.

Corporate Protection against Adversity

As in the case of the cornfield mentioned earlier, symbiotic community provides protection from the storms that threaten it. There is power in numbers, and Jesus told us that where two or three are gathered in his name, he is there also (Matt. 18:20). When we gather in his name, we have each other, but more than that, we experience a more evident presence of God.

Like many of the western states, Idaho is fighting endless battles against the intrusion of encroaching noxious weeds. In Idaho alone we now have fifty-two different species of weeds that are taking over our pastures and grazing lands and threatening our ability to feed domestic stock and wildlife. A number of organizations have taken up the fight against this very present and threatening enemy. Thousands of dollars are being spent to combat this destructive foe in what can only be labeled as a war to protect our land.

Here on Timber Butte we fight a number of these encroaching weed species, one of which we refer to as skeletonweed. It is not good to find skeletonweed growing on the land—once it gets a foothold, it is nearly impossible to eradicate. Only very powerful poison herbicide sprays will combat it. Unfortunately, such chemicals kill good vegetation along with the weeds and over time penetrate deep into both soil and groundwater.

Skeletonweed is so pervasive because it sends down long roots deep into the soil and can sustain itself in any climate more readily than the natural foliage. Last year I noticed that it was becoming established in one of our hay fields, which really alarmed me. We had avoided using chemicals for weed abatement so I wasn't quite sure what I should do to get rid of it. I knew I couldn't hand pull three acres of deep-rooted weeds, and mowing them only stimulates greater growth, much like pruning a tree. I remember a statement John Wimber, the founder of the Vineyard Movement, once said concerning spiritual warfare—one of the best ways to overcome evil is to crowd it out with goodness. With that in mind, I decided to replant the field with a type of barley grass that thrives in our area, in hopes of overwhelming the skeletonweed with a good crop. It worked, and the noxious weeds were literally crowded out by a thick stand of healthy barley.

As Christian believers, we are called to be a community that grows up in the midst of a broken and pain-filled culture. We may not be of the world but we are clearly living in it—a world pervaded with many evils that are antagonistic toward our efforts to live righteous, Christlike lives. The Lord's desire and our responsibility is not to go around pulling out weeds of unrighteousness, but rather to crowd out the evil with healthy, thriving communities of grace, mercy, and compassion. Paul put it this way:

> Do not repay anyone evil for evil. Be careful to do what is right in the eyes of everybody. If it is possible, as far as it depends on you, live at peace with everyone. Do not take revenge, my friends, but leave room for God's wrath, for it is written: "It is mine to avenge; I will repay," says the Lord. On the contrary: "If your enemy is hungry, feed him; if he is thirsty, give him something to drink. In doing this, you will heap burning coals on his head." Do not be overcome by evil, but overcome evil with good.
>
> Romans 12:17–21

When our fellowship first moved onto the twenty-two acres of property that we now call our permanent home, we found ourselves in the middle of one of the least desirable areas of our city. Although it was only minutes from Boise's downtown center, our community was known as Garden City. Garden City was anything but a garden. Its crime rate in those days was the highest in the entire state of Idaho, and the main street was known for its adult pornography shops, grungy bars, and motels that advertised rooms that could be rented for an hour at a time. Per capita, there were more registered sexual offenders living within a mile of our new church site than any other part of our state. The very arguments against this being a desirable place to live were the reasons we decided to relocate in Garden City—we wanted to be where we believed Jesus would want to be.

We never protested the immorality or came against the corruptness of our new community; rather, we simply served. To the best of our ability we blessed our neighborhood with kindness and goodness. As we walked its streets, we discovered cases of extreme poverty in the blocks that surrounded us. Many of the residents lived in dilapidated, old trailer homes, many of which had cardboard-covered broken windows and yards that were littered and unkempt. One Thanksgiving we went door-to-door giving away free turkeys only to discover that many of the inhabitants didn't have a way of cooking them. We also gave away twenty-five-dollar food vouchers until we could eventually build the benevolence center and free medical clinic that so effectively serve the community today.

> *Symbiotic communities always have positive benefits in the environments they inhabit, whether in the plant world, physical world, or spiritual world.*

We don't try to take credit for the many changes that have taken place, but today Garden City is a different place than it was fifteen years ago. The grimy motels, grungy bars, and adult bookstores have disappeared one by one, and the culture and reputation of the area have dramatically improved. The city hall and the local police department have both acknowledged our presence as having played a role in the changes.

Symbiotic communities always have positive benefits in the environments they inhabit, whether in the plant world, physical world, or spiritual world.

Sustainable Regeneration

Symbiotic communities are able to regenerate themselves. God has programmed all of nature for sustainable reproduction and regeneration. At the end of a harvest or growing season, new seed is broadcast in preparation for the season to come. This must be true of the church as well.

Having become more aware of techniques in organic gardening in recent years, we have discovered the advantages of using heirloom rather than the standard F1 hybrid vegetable seeds sold in most stores across America. We had always used hybrid seed before, not knowing there was a difference. Hybrid seed is genetically altered to produce specifically desired results, but it is only functional for the production of one generation. The seed that is developed in the fruits or vegetables is sterile and thus incapable of reproducing a second generation. By comparison, heirloom seeds grow fruit that contains seeds capable of bearing new generations of fruit or vegetables season after season. Major corporations have attempted to wean farmers and gardeners off heirloom seeds to create annual dependency on the products these companies market.

In a way it might be said that hybrid seeds are to the plant world what mules are to the animal world. They have great value for one generation, but when their life is over, their breed ends with them. A mule is the end result of crossing a horse with a donkey, and much like hybrid seed, a mule is sterile and unable to reproduce a second generation. Mules are specially bred for their calm disposition, endurance, and strength. They have great value as long as there are people who are deliberately manipulating the crossbreeding of these two different species. If the world became dependent on mules for survival, mule breeders would have a controlled corner on the market, as mules do not naturally reproduce on their own. American agriculture is rapidly falling into this same kind of dependency. If farmers use only hybrid seed, they cannot produce their own seed for the next season of planting, which generations of farmers have done before them.

We must pass the life we have discovered in Christ from one generation to the next.

We Christians are meant to be like heirloom seed. We too must pass the life we have discovered in Christ from one generation to the next. The older generation must not only want to pass this new life on but be purposeful and even deliberate about doing so. It's no secret that today the American church is growing older. Year by year there seems to be more and more gray hair in the pews as many Christian denominations gradually lose ground in attendance and energy. Even the most thriving mega churches across the country are being led by baby boomers who are now in their fifties and sixties. For the church to be sustainable, there must be a changing of the guard. It is time to become symbiotic communities programmed to regenerate through the raising and empowering of a new generation for leadership.

Investing in Community

Three years ago Nancy and I woke up early one morning long before daylight and sat looking out our front window, reminiscing about how much God had blessed our ministry experience through our thirty years of leadership. We recalled how we had received the vision twenty years earlier to plant a new church in Boise, and how that prompted us to leave our ranch in California to become reestablished in Idaho in 1989. We remembered the sacrifices and joys we had experienced as we chose to take one of the greatest steps of faith we ever had, risking our security and the security of the families who had decided to join us. That quiet morning, sitting there together in the dark, we looked back with gratitude while embracing some courageous choices we had to make concerning our future ministry life as well.

Back in 1988, having been entrenched as leaders for so long in the Lancaster church, we decided not to advertise our intentions of moving to Idaho for fear of disrupting the fellowship. We knew we were loved in our church community and decided to quietly prepare for our new adventure in Boise, only announcing it within an inner circle of leaders until our time of departure. Things have a way of seeping out, however, and soon families started to approach us announcing that they wanted to join us in our new adventure. Most of them hadn't even been to Idaho and chose to follow us only because they believed Nancy and I had an authentic vision from the Lord to plant the church.

During the following summer of 1989, vehicle after vehicle of our church planting team drove more than eight hundred miles across the deserts of eastern California, the entire length of Nevada, and the southeastern corner of Oregon until they finally crossed the state line into Idaho. Twelve families had given up their jobs, sold their homes, and said good-bye to family and friends to become established in a city where they knew no one. What they did was both sacrificial and courageous, and knowing this sobered me with a deep sense of responsibility as there wasn't any guarantee that our new church venture would succeed.

Nancy and I had experienced community before this to some degree, but this was at an altogether different level. We became a people much like the first-century church that had been drawn together not so much by previous relationship but by vision and a sense of divine purpose. We were so motivated by the dream of what we were about to do that the fear of failure and the discomfort of sacrifice were overshadowed by optimistic expectation. We were having fun and we were having it together.

Every time a new family arrived in Boise, others would meet them, helping unload moving vans, trucks, and trailers and assisting them in the hunt for a home. Some of the families camped in the backyards of others as they searched for jobs and places to live. People cooked and ate meals together and helped each other get established. We painted each other's homes and cleaned up yards. This activity went on throughout the summer of 1989, but when September arrived, we held our first official meetings as a church planting team. In the beginning we met two nights a week in a small office complex we had rented, spending our time praying, worshiping, and strategizing to establish the new work.

Working Together

By November of that fall, we had made our first move into a small, vacated community church, which was located only minutes from the downtown city center. We joined together with one heart and mind, pooling what money we had to paint the small inside meeting room and clean up the outside of the facility. We pieced together a makeshift but adequate sound system, set up two small Sunday school rooms with flimsy plastic furniture, and announced our first official service.

The Boise Vineyard had been birthed by a small ragtag bunch of believers who had chosen to trust God and serve in his kingdom. All of us had to play a part—in fact everyone played several significant parts. Participation was not an option in those first days as everyone took on some form of ministry, according to their diverse gifts.

It was decided that we would all have a role on Sunday, either being on the worship team, working with the children, greeting, making coffee, or whatever else was needed. In addition to Sunday morning, everyone also played a part in a midweek home group, either opening their home to host a small group or facilitating the evening's inductive Bible study. Everyone got involved—some would lead the worship while others even helped with childcare. The entire church planting team was required to attend a leadership meeting at our home every Saturday morning. In those early days, we considered everyone a leader.

We all felt a deep sense of privilege to be a part of something God was so obviously blessing, and because of this feeling, the commitment level was very high. Honestly, the community life we were experiencing was so unique and rich that the expectation and excitement we felt kept us motivated even when things got difficult. (Our first food bank was started in an effort to feed our church planting team.) And in the midst of our struggles, the Lord continually added to our numbers, bringing us new families and singles week after week, and our new little church began to grow.

One of the amazing things that enabled our fellowship to function was having the blessing of a full-time professional yet volunteer church staff. On the same property as our first church facility, there was a small house that once served as a pastor's parsonage. As our church grew, our monthly finances enabled us to rent and convert it into a makeshift office. Sharon Taylor and Lori Thompson were wives in two of our church planting families. Both of their husbands had found employment in the valley and encouraged them to volunteer as full-time workers. They had both previously worked with me to establish an elementary school program in California. That first year they served faithfully without pay as secretaries, administrative assistants, and even the cleaning crew.

Another very significant part of that first church staff was Ruben Navarrete. Ruben was a single twenty-one-year-old who had helped me in California with a youth ministry called the God Rock Café. Ruben had spent time working in Africa with Youth With A Mission and, although young, he had excelled as a real estate agent in Southern California. This enabled Ruben to put aside a financial nest egg, which he used to support himself while serving as the church's first volunteer business manager. He set up our 501C3 nonprofit corporation, kept the books, and negotiated for our first facility leases and our eventual property purchase.

In those first days, all of us worked as if we were receiving a full salary, believing there might be a day we actually would. Today, twenty years later, Sharon and Lori are still faithfully serving on the church staff, and Ruben (now married and the father of a young son) is fully engaged as a volunteer resource and is an incredible support to me.

Diversity and Cooperation

As the church grew, it became more and more dynamic. It didn't take long before it began reaching out into the community and eventually into the world in very tangible ways.

Over time some of our original church planting team moved on to do other types of ministry, some joining new, smaller church planting efforts. In some respects I think they may have missed the tight-knit community life of those early entrepreneurial days. Yet many stayed and have become fully engaged in the ministry, even though our culture has shifted as the church has grown. As the Lord gave new growth, we had to grow with it and that meant changes. We could no longer focus only on our original small community; we needed to open our lives up to embrace the hundreds of new people who began to join us.

As the church community grew, so did the diversity of gifting. New ministries started to emerge and expand, reaching into dozens of subcultures, such as children, youth, young adults, the elderly, recovering addicts, the poor, men's and women's groups, and prisoners. We were able to use people in their passions and callings to do vast varieties of unique ministry in our city, the nation, and the world. We sent teams to work in the aftermath of natural disasters, to start a free medical clinic, to address areas of social crises and injustice such as human trafficking, the environment, and illiteracy. More than a hundred people even joined together in a ministry of the visual arts, which continually blesses the church and provides it with resources through creative expression.

The work of the church expanded, and in the first five years we moved four times until we finally purchased a twenty-two-acre plot of land where we are currently developing an expansive church campus. As our facilities grew, so did our community of believers. We gathered in multiple services on Sundays, and soon Nancy and I struggled to remember the names of our people or what was going on in the vast amount of ministry that had emerged. During this time of growth, we realized we would have to sacrifice having the kind of personal relationships we once had with everyone who called our church "home."

The community had changed, but it continued to grow in its symbiotic nature and function. Within the community there were dozens of smaller groups—like-hearted, like-minded people who worked together in areas that needed their diverse gifts and passions. Ministries, although very different in nature, encouraged and supported one another. The environmental ministry worked with the women's ministry team teaching classes on gardening and sustainable living techniques. The art community helped draw wall murals in the halls of the children's ministry and the nursery, and the kitchen crew that cooked dinner every Friday night for two hundred folks in the drug and alcohol recovery program volunteered to prepare a huge steak dinner for a young adults' special event. The missions ministry joined forces with the social justice ministries, taking their trained medical team to the extreme poor in developing nations. Cross-pollination started to happen everywhere, and as a result, our work became far more productive as deep, new, lasting relationships emerged. We had become a thriving symbiotic community in the truest sense.

Regeneration

That early morning as Nancy and I sat there recounting all the ways the Lord had been so good to us through the work of the church, we sensed this community of believers had yet one more thing to accomplish to become truly symbiotic. We had to be sure that the church community we worked so hard to build would be regenerated like the heirloom seeds. Somehow we had to successfully pass the church on to the emerging generation. We needed to step aside, give up our positions as senior pastors, and encourage the younger generation to rise up and lead. We had enjoyed the privilege of participating in a first wave of growth and harvest, but if the next wave was to come, we had to get out of the way somehow and allow the new seed to break forth and develop into fully mature leaders. In truth this was a very hard reality to face—perhaps the hardest yet.

In recent years we have been surrounded by numbers of gifted young leaders; many have been in the church for years and have grown into healthy committed adults. We are proud of them and have learned to trust in their wisdom and abilities—it would be to these that our spiritual inheritance would be passed on.

What has transpired from our decision that early morning is worthy of a book of its own, but I will say that it has propelled us into a rich but stretching transitional season. As a result of our commitment to the emerging generation and the ongoing fruitful work of our church, we have come to believe this may be the most important decision we have ever made. Neither Nancy nor I feel like retiring, backing off from ministry, or withdrawing in any way. We have more vision, credibility, authority to speak, and energy to lead today than ever before. We have no intention of leaving our church fellowship, but we are fully committed to taking a backseat for the purpose of allowing a new gifted generation of leaders to step up to the plate. We are grateful for those new leaders and are grooming them in the process.

You might say it is our desire to take grandparent roles while we still have the energy to roll around on the floor with the kids. We believe our decision to invest seriously in the emerging generation is the hope for the ongoing health and sustainability of our now thriving symbiotic community.

8

The Thrill of the Harvest

Bearing Fruit

Growing a healthy bumper crop for harvest is as much an art form as it is science. Farming demands a passion to create, and this is equally as important as the know-how for growing things. It requires a love and willingness for hard work, gratitude for God's provision, and a love for the gift and miracle of the earth's soil. I have been pondering the concept that working the land somehow taps into and touches a hidden strand of ancient DNA that God placed in the human spirit for a purpose greater than growing fruits and vegetables.

Source of Fulfillment

I believe successful farming requires not only the rooting of various plant species but also getting in touch with the very roots of human existence—realizing that all of humanity began with one lone couple who were called to tend a garden that God had established. Genesis records: "Now the LORD God had planted a garden in the east, in Eden; and there he put the man he had formed. And the LORD God made all kinds of trees grow out of the ground— trees that were pleasing to the eye and good for food. . . . The LORD God took the man and put him in the Garden of Eden to work it and take care of it" (Gen. 2:8–9, 15). Humankind was created with a built-in love and even a drive to participate in the thrill of harvest; it has been in us all from the very beginning of time. My premise, then, is that everyone has been called to plant and harvest in one form or another; and because of it, bearing fruit in our lives is the only thing that really satisfies our deep need for human fulfillment.

I've watched Nancy come alive this summer as she labors in our vegetable garden. She and Lily, our small golden Lab, spend hours together day after day planting, carefully cultivating between rows, watering, and pulling undesired weeds, with the anticipation of a fruitful future harvest. Our garden is now becoming bountiful and beautiful, and it is actually having the same effect on Nancy. It is medicine to her soul and a sedative of peace to calm any fears or restless emotions. More than a plot of dirt, a garden is a place of healing, renewal, and expectant vision. It is a picture of the kingdom of God and provides a very tangible means of learning about it.

The Bible tells us that the natural things of creation speak of the unseen supernatural world, as inferred in Romans 1:20. It would then make perfect sense that the things we see and experience in a natural garden parallel things God desires for us on a spiritual level. Because of his deep love for us, God desperately wants us rooted and established in his love—the Father's love. His desire is for us to mature and grow in strength under the warmth and in the light of his Son, and to experience the refreshment and power of the Spirit's rain. God made us for his spiritual garden, a garden that would one day be used in the process of producing a great harvest of human souls.

We started tilling up the ground in our garden at Timber Butte in early spring, just after the winter's snowpack had surrendered to the spring rains. The days had gradually grown longer and held a promise of warmer weather to come. The ground seemed lifeless and cold at that time, a long way from being ready to produce anything. There were no hopeful signs of growth, no outward appearance of the future yield. Yet the thought of beautiful, blossoming plants and ripened vegetables motivated us to labor on, even with the knowledge that it would be months before we gleaned the benefits of harvest.

Ready Laborers

Gardening is about vision. It requires the ability to sacrifice and patiently wait for the fruit of an unseen future. Gardening requires faith to believe that God in his grace will again breathe life into a small seed lying in darkness beneath the surface of cultivated, composted dirt.

As the summer days grew longer and warmer at Timber Butte, the wait for the harvest was over—the garden began to produce more vegetables than we could possibly eat ourselves. The challenge was no longer waiting for the crop to grow, but harvesting and blessing others with its bounty before it became too ripe.

In the business of gardening, timing and working with the desire to benefit others are keys to success; and so it is with the harvest Jesus spoke of when he said, "The harvest is plentiful but the workers are few. Ask the Lord of the harvest, therefore, to send out workers into his harvest field" (Matt. 9:37–38). Jesus's words are clearly spoken with a sense of kingdom urgency, which can only be understood if we grasp the context in which he was speaking. Throughout Matthew 9 Jesus had been ministering and demonstrating the kingdom of God's presence everywhere he went. He had been healing some who were blind and mute, delivering others from demons, and forgiving those who were caught in lives of sin, such as when he ate with Matthew the tax collector in his home. Throughout his ministry on earth, Jesus's heart was full of compassion for broken humanity.

The Scripture tells us that Jesus had been going through all the towns and villages, "teaching in their synagogues, preaching the good news of the kingdom and healing every disease and sickness" (v. 35). Then it says, "When he saw the crowds, he had compassion on them, because they were harassed and helpless, like sheep without a shepherd" (v. 36). Only after these words did Jesus exhort his disciples, saying, "The harvest is plentiful but the workers are few." His motivation for calling disciples to the harvest was the brokenness of the human race. He saw people harassed, helpless, and aimless and in desperate need of a shepherd who could care for and guide them.

If the brokenness of the human race is the criteria by which we can determine the ripeness of harvest, then I believe we would all admit that the harvest is ready; and honestly that really isn't the issue. The issue is more about those of us who are called to do the labor of bringing in the harvest. The work requires mature Christian disciples. In Jesus's parable of the harvest, disciples are those who have been harvested and are now called to harvest others. Harvesters are those of us who have gone through the growth process, reached some level of authentic maturity, and become passionate to see others do the same. Harvesters have experienced the grace of God, know the truth about his eternal kingdom, and share in his compassion for the millions of people who are about to miss heaven. They are people who by faith have become so convinced of the reality of God's existence that they are ready to give their lives as laborers in his fields.

Humanity's Impending Destruction

Years ago when I was in my early twenties, I wrote my master's thesis on the American West. Specifically, I concentrated on the Big Sky Country, which today would include Idaho, Montana, and Wyoming. I loved studying the development of the West, especially during the era of the mountain men, beginning with Lewis and Clark through the time of the trappers.

I was fascinated with the Indian tribes of the Upper Plains regions, such as the Crow, the Sioux, the Shoshone, and the Blackfoot. It amazed me how the Native Americans survived so well through the long winters in such a harsh climate with only primitive weaponry to help them gather their necessary large reserves of winter meat. One of the primary ways the Blackfoot did this was by driving entire buffalo herds off cliffs. The Blackfoot tribe called it a "buffalo jump" or "pishkun." For hundreds of years they used this technique as a means of harvesting buffalo meat, hides for shelter and clothing, and bones for tools.

The Indians would stack rocks into tall piles called "dead men" out in the open plains. The first piles were placed close together near the cliff's edge, with more piles stacked about a hundred yards apart in a funnel-like fashion extending some eight miles outward. When a large herd of buffalo grazed through the area, Indian hunters would put on animal skin robes, disguising themselves as wolves and other animals in hopes of deceiving the herd. They would crawl close to the outside of the herd and in unison jump up and scare the buffalo in the direction of the pishkun rock funnel. Other hunters hidden behind the dead men rock piles would then jump up waving blankets as the herd passed by, causing the buffalo to frantically run down the funnel toward the cliff's edge until they started to cascade over to their ultimate destruction. From the time I became a Christian, I have thought of this practice of mass panic and death as a vivid illustration of humanity aimlessly running toward destruction.

If we are to join Christ in a great eternal harvest, we must first have a revelation of heaven and of hell. We must be awakened to the reality that man is destined to rush headlong over the cliffs of destruction unless he is turned onto God's path of salvation through Christ. When Paul wrote to the Colossians, he spoke of this rescue from the cliff's edge when he said, "For he has rescued us from the dominion of darkness and brought us into the kingdom of the Son he loves, in whom we have redemption, the forgiveness of sins" (Col. 1:13–14).

Even as you are reading these words, masses of people all over the world are cascading off the edge of natural life into an eternity of doom because no one shouted a warning and presented the option that could have saved them. No one told them to turn around and head away from destruction toward a new life with God.

The word *repentance* means to turn around and head in a different direction. In the second chapter of Acts, after the people of Jerusalem heard the gospel preached, the Scripture says, "They were cut to the heart and said to Peter and the other apostles, 'Brothers, what shall we do?' " (v. 37). Peter's response to them was: "Repent and be baptized, every one of you, in the name of Jesus Christ for the forgiveness of your sins" (v. 38). Salvation begins with the recognition that we are living a life of running away from God and we must change course or we will miss his blessing (but not the cliff!).

The devil is the enemy of humanity. He is a deceiver that can take on many disguises, but his ultimate intention is to get entire nations, cultures, and societies to run en masse toward hell—his own destination. His goal is our death and destruction—and much like the buffalo herds, masses of people are running toward an eternal cliff without even knowing what awaits them at the end.

When Jesus calls us to the harvest, he calls us to stand in front of the charging herd of humanity with our arms waving and our mouths shouting the truth concerning what lies ahead of them. This action is called the proclamation of the gospel and it requires extreme courage, courage that can and will only be motivated by authentic faith. This is the final role of a seed that has been planted and come to full spiritual maturity. This is the ultimate purpose of the discipling harvester.

Compassion for the Harvest

Jesus's motivation for calling for harvesters was his deep love for humanity. If it is true that we have been created like the first man, Adam, to become harvesters, and if our harvest field is the sea of humanity who need to know Jesus, then we must somehow capture God's heart of love for a world that is broken and in deep physical and spiritual crisis. Obviously this can happen differently for everyone, but for me it became evident in two very clear ways.

Witnessing the Brokenness

The first was accomplished through getting me out of my comfort zone and into opportunities to experience broken humanity firsthand. Over the years, God has given me the privilege and opportunity to get out into the harvest fields of the world and experience the reality of the human condition. I have seen the devastating results of AIDS in Africa, the despair of ethnic cleansing in Burma, the hopelessness of extreme poverty fueled by corrupt leadership and governments in various nations of South America, and the result of spiritual complacency in Europe and North America. I have been among the affluent and the extreme

146

poor on nearly every continent, and it is through these experiences that I have become aware of a world that is spiritually bankrupt. It has broken me and driven me to cry out to God for a part to play in the solution.

Ministering to the Least of These

The second way I came to understand God's heart started one day when I was reading the book of Isaiah. It was one of those times when the Scripture comes alive and jumps off the page into your heart—and it transformed my worldview and my understanding of who I was as a Christian. A short journey through the Scriptures gave me a passion to do more with my life than I had been doing up to that point.

Much of the book of Isaiah is recorded prophecy concerning the coming Messiah. It was written some eight hundred years before Jesus's appearance on the earth and describes in great detail the characteristics of a Messiah who would one day appear, bringing provision for the salvation of humanity. God told the prophet that mankind would know the Messiah when he came because he would do certain things and possess specific attributes that would characterize his true spiritual leadership. He would have a heart for the poor and would bring authentic healing to the broken. He would provide freedom to those who had been held captive. He would provide comfort for those who mourn, and turn the ashes of broken lives to crowns of beauty, and spirits of despair to garments of gladness and praise (see Isaiah 61:1–3). Isaiah said that when the true Messiah showed up, he would be a prince of peace offering salvation and redemption to lost humanity.

From there the journey through Scripture took me to the Gospel of Luke, chapter 4, in which Luke records the events right before Jesus's public ministry really began. Jesus had just spent forty days and nights in the wilderness when he returned to his hometown of Nazareth. He returned on the Sabbath and, as was his custom, he entered the synagogue. The Scripture tells us that the attendant handed him the scroll of Isaiah, and he opened it to this clearly messianic passage and read it before all who were present, saying, "Today this scripture is fulfilled in your hearing" (v. 21) or, in other words, "I'm the one!—I'm the Messiah for whom you have been looking and waiting." This of course outraged those who had known him from childhood, but the fact remained: he was the one, and his life did reflect all of the prophecy that had been spoken about him. Over the course of the next three years, Jesus did minister to the least of the least. He lived among the poor and the downtrodden, proclaiming the kingdom of God and bringing both evidence and assurance of its presence through miracles of healing and deliverance.

Three years later, only hours before the arrest that would take him to the cross, Jesus sat on a hillside outside of Jerusalem with his inner circle of disciples, telling them about the events of the final days before his second coming. It was here, as recorded in Matthew 24, that Jesus described a world and humanity that were in a state of extreme crisis. He said there would be an escalation of world violence—wars and rumors of wars. He also described an increase of natural disasters, famines, and world hunger; an increase of disease and plague; and a breakdown of social and ethical values that would cause the love of many to grow cold. In a nutshell, all of humanity would be in a state of suffering, especially the extreme poor. He said that these last days would be like the days of Noah when people wouldn't listen to warnings but continued to carry on their lives, ignoring the world's increasingly desperate, decaying condition.

As he concluded this end-time dissertation, he told three consecutive parables, all of which communicate a message of the urgent need for faithfulness and stewardship before his second coming. It was here that he told the story of an unfaithful steward who didn't care for his master's estate in his absence. Here also is found the tale of the three servants who were given various sums of money or talents to invest, not knowing at what hour their master would return. In each case they were judged according to how faithful they were in their master's absence. Their individual degree of faithfulness determined their eternal outcome. Their actions were a revelation of their level of confidence in his second coming.

In my journey of reading through these Scriptures, I came to the awareness that it is only authentic faith that will determine how we respond to a desperate world that is becoming increasingly unraveled and devastated by crises. It is not coincidence that in the very next chapter (Matthew 25), Jesus spoke of the separation of all mankind at his final judgment based on this response. It was here that he said, "All the nations will be gathered in his presence, and he will separate the people as a shepherd separates the sheep from the goats. He will place the sheep at his right hand and the goats at his left" (vv. 32–33 NLT). The story continues:

Then the King will say to those on his right, "Come, you who are blessed by my Father, inherit the Kingdom prepared for you from the creation of the world. For I was hungry, and you fed me. I was thirsty, and you gave me a drink. I was a stranger, and you invited me into your home. I was naked, and you gave me clothing. I was sick, and you cared for me. I was in prison, and you visited me."

verses 34–36 NLT

Jesus's disciples asked him when any of these things ever happened to him—being naked, hungry, thirsty, sick, a stranger, or in prison—and he simply responded, "When you did it to one of the least of these my brothers and sisters, you were doing it to me!" (v. 40 NLT). He has called us to minister and harvest in the midst of escalating world crises, especially among the very people the prophet Isaiah said he would deliver from oppression and pain—the extreme poor and distressed.

Regaining Our Zeal

In the spring of 2009 I received a phone call from an old friend in Portland. I'd known Glenn Schroder for nearly thirty years from my early days of ministry in Southern California. When I first met Glenn, he was the youth pastor at the Anaheim Vineyard, but he had later moved to the Northwest to plant a church in Oregon. Glenn had joined two other old ministry friends of mine, Roy Conwell and Steve Fish, to establish a missions partnership in Nicaragua. I had not been in contact with any of them for quite a while, but I was aware of their efforts in Central America.

Actually I had very little knowledge of what they were really up to there, but I knew, with their adventurous spirits and unique personalities, it must be something good. I had had the privilege of going on ministry trips with Roy in the past. During one of those trips, we rode on a riverboat down the Amazon River and up the Shingo River, visiting villages and preaching in young churches along the way. On another occasion we took our two sons into New Orleans the week after Hurricane Katrina had devastated the region. We spent days cutting huge oak trees off houses and out of roadways in an effort to give people access back into the city and to their homes.

Steve Fish had quite a story of his own. He was one of the original leaders of the Jesus Movement. At the time— the sixties and seventies—he was a long-haired hippie who came to Christ in the heat of the revival. Along with his wife, Layne, he had helped run Christian communes up and down the coast of California.

When Glenn called with a request for me to teach a conference their partnership was hosting in Nicaragua, I was buried up to my neck in life. We were going through a major transition in our church; Nancy and I were in the midst of developing Timber Butte; I was trying desperately to meet a deadline for a book manuscript; and we were in the middle of helping our kids navigate through some very difficult marriage problems. To say the least, life was crazy.

So my first reaction to Glenn's proposal for me to join him, Roy, and Steve on their ministry trip was to decline. I honestly felt too tired and too overwhelmed to add another stick to a fire I felt was already burning out of control. Knowing Glenn wouldn't make it easy on me to back off, I told him I would look over my calendar, talk to Nancy, and pray about it. In my mind this was another way of saying, "I'll tell you no later."

The problem was that I did pray about it, and in doing so I felt a deep conviction from the Lord that I should go. What Glenn had asked me to do was a real honor. For six years these three leaders and their churches had made a joint effort to build an orphanage and plant half a dozen indigenous churches throughout the country of Nicaragua. This conference, though small, would represent the first national gathering of these new churches in one place at one time. Glenn asked me to teach for three days on the kingdom of God. In my prayer time, the Lord reminded me that there was no greater privilege than to teach about his kingdom to the nations. How could I refuse when this was the very thing I signed up to do so many years before?

There are many reasons we lose our zeal as harvesters, but offhand I can think of three. The first is that we lose sight of the reality of eternity; we simply don't believe in it enough to risk standing in front of a herd of charging buffalo. This is like the seed in the parable that is lost due to unbelief. Satan, like birds, picks it away.

The second reason we lose our zeal is that we become distracted by life's problems and grow weary of conflict, losing sight of God's provision of inner peace. This is like the seed that falls on the rocky soil. Its roots never get fully established.

The third reason is that in our humanness we have a tendency to take our eyes off God's will and onto our own stuff. The things of the world are constantly at work luring us toward false promises of security, comfort, and pleasure. We get our eyes on ourselves and lose our passion to make a difference with our lives. This is like the seed that falls in the thistles and thorns. In the end we lose sight of God's heart and simply don't care what happens to other people. I can personally relate to all of these follies, and on this particular occasion with Glenn's invitation before me, I nearly missed a life-changing opportunity to serve the Lord and share in his harvest field.

Renewing Our Heart

It was an early July morning when Nancy took me to the airport to catch the plane to Managua, the capital of Nicaragua. I felt depressed knowing that I would be away from home again after traveling so much already that year. I had never been to Nicaragua but knew about its slow recovery from a devastating revolution under the leadership of a corrupt dictator. I was seriously weary and not feeling on top of my game. The truth is, I just didn't feel that I had much to give. Yet I desperately didn't want to disappoint my old friends who were depending on me.

The plane landed late that evening, and after clearing customs, I was immediately comforted as I recognized those crazy, smiling faces through the terminal windows in the midst of the chaotic crowd. After some brief hugging and handshaking in the humid tropical air, we loaded into a van and headed an hour out of the city to the orphanage they had all worked hard to establish. On the way they shared what they had been doing through

In the end we lose sight of God's heart and simply don't care what happens to other people.

the missions partnership, and about the political, social, and economic condition of Nicaragua. I learned that the unemployment rate was over 50 percent, and the extreme poverty that resulted was having a devastating ripple effect on a country that had once been considered one of the wealthiest in Central America.

Since I had arrived early for the conference, I had the chance to hang out with my old comrades and experience what they had been doing. One day they took me to visit the Managua city dump, which provides trash disposal for some two million people. Visiting a dump in a developing nation isn't something most tourists would do; but if you want to discover the truth about a society's condition, it is the most revealing place to begin. It tells the story of the cycle of poverty in a way that would both shock and devastate people who aren't spiritually prepared to see it.

As heartbreaking as it is, what I saw that day in Managua is not unique; it is a scenario that is reproduced in nearly every city in the developing nations of the world. Thousands of people literally spend their entire lives in these dumps, some never even seeing the outside world. This is their entire life and livelihood. Their houses are built from what can be salvaged from the refuse; their food comes from its waste; and whatever income they make comes from cashing in and recycling the debris.

We stood on a hill that rose above a landscape of mile after mile of garbage, observing truck after truck dump its towering load. With every load, literally hundreds of people—men, women, and children—stormed the trucks hoping to be the first to extract the precious resources that the rest of their society considered useless garbage. We were told that it wasn't uncommon for people in their zeal for trash to lose their lives after becoming buried under the discarded piles of rubble.

Watching from our vantage point, it made me think of what hell must be like. Here and there methane gas pockets erupted in flames, which was another common source of devastating injury or death to the people who inhabited that place. Everything was polluted far beyond anything I had ever seen. Children swam and bathed in a small lake that not only was surrounded by trash but had decaying rubbish floating in it. As I viewed the hopeless scene before me, God was rebreaking and renewing my heart for suffering humanity. He was reminding me again that I couldn't hide behind busyness, life's commotion, or extreme weariness. I had to do something. I could never cease being an active participant in his kingdom. I could not give up. I had to collect myself and muster up the courage by his Spirit to continue running the race to the end.

Recognizing the Field

When I first became aware of the statistics for extreme poverty, they didn't really affect me because the crises in the world seemed so far removed. But the numbers are real and they expose the condition of real people, many of whom are innocent children. They reveal the ominous gap between the world's rich and poor that is drastically widening. Before our latest national recession, the average family in America made approximately $55,000 a year, while nearly half the world's population lives on less than $2 a day (or approximately $730 a year). According to one

United Nations report, there are presently 200 million children living and working in the streets. Other reports estimate that in today's world, 2.5 billion people (one-third of the world's population) do not have access to clean, drinkable water. They go on to report that polluted water is responsible for 80 percent of all illness and death in the developing world, killing a child every 8 seconds, and that more than 2 billion people are presently starving worldwide while another 2 billion are malnourished. Poverty creates a vicious cycle of physical pain, hopelessness, and despair. People who are caught in it see no way out until someone brings them a message of hope and a means to both spiritual and physical freedom. This then is the harvest field to which God has called us. From my experience, it is a field of hope as well as great joy and unbelievable fulfillment.

Before we can break the cycle of poverty, we have to understand that it is not so much a cycle but a downward spiral. Often the spiral begins with corrupt leadership—leadership that is either self-promoting and uncaring about the condition of the people, or has bought into an ideology that leads away from Christlikeness. Either way it is ungodly and spiritually bankrupt. When God is removed, so is the blessing that once caused society to prosper. The downward spiral begins.

As the economy depresses and inflates, people lose their livelihood, forcing them to find other more desperate means of survival. Historically, they have turned on the land itself. When people are desperate to feed their families, the ideals of environmental stewardship vanish and the land becomes abused beyond sustainability. Trees are cut down for fuel and timber, causing topsoil to erode, being washed away by unrestrained runoff. Then the land loses its ability to produce crops. The conditions of poverty and hunger are exacerbated and people become vulnerable to disease and domestic violence. Often children are the ones who suffer the most. Instead of being able to attend school, they are forced to help the family survive. Illiteracy increases.

With the lack of even the most basic necessities of survival, these conditions lead to a hotbed of unrest with theft, more violent crimes, and even political upheaval, which often means a more oppressive government. Then the population becomes even more repressed and oppressed. Desperate people end up doing desperate things—even to the point of selling their young children into prostitution. In the midst of its despair, the society loses its moral compass. Diseases such as AIDS rise to epidemic levels. And again the children suffer, losing their parents and ending up in orphanages or on the streets where they are easy prey to the atrocities of the sex trade or child soldiering. It is estimated that nearly ten million children are victims in today's international sex slave industry.

Two years ago Nancy and I went to Zambia, Africa, along with our missions director and a few others from our church. Invited by Kirk Schauer, founder of a ministry called Seeds of Hope, we went with the plan to set up a long-term ministry base in an extremely poor community near the city of Ndola. The primary objective of Seeds of Hope is to drill wells and produce water filters in poverty-stricken areas. Seeing this work gave us a whole new meaning to Jesus's statement: "I was thirsty and you gave me something to drink" (Matt. 25:35). I understood how providing clean water to thirsty people is a means of ministering to Jesus and what he meant when he said, "Whatever you did for one of the least of these brothers of mine, you did it for me" (v. 40). I also realized just how real the downward spiral of a society is. Yet in the midst of it all, there is great hope—and that hope is the church. As Christians all over the world capture the heart of God for the poor and broken, recognize the commission of Jesus, and respond in unity, these atrocious conditions can and will begin to change.

Every time I find myself in the middle of poverty and crises, I see Christians serving on the front lines. I have been in the refugee camps of Thailand, where Christians are teaching English and providing physical relief. In the slums of Cebu and Manila it is young, trained Christian women who are providing midwifery services to the poor, elevating the survival rate of many women and babies in these places. In the ghettos of Paraguay, Christians are ministering in the narrow streets and shanties. It is the church that is bringing hope to so much of Africa as Christian workers minister to AIDS victims and address issues of crisis and poverty. While in Ecuador recently, Nancy and I were moved to tears as we witnessed Christian workers running an orphanage for dozens of Downs syndrome and seriously disabled babies—babies who had been abandoned and discarded on the streets. Even in my visit to the dump of Managua, I saw Christians serving meals to the children under a hot, dilapidated military tent, and young volunteers were playing soccer with the teens amidst the horrible smells and the stifling heat.

Here's the bottom line. One-third of the world's population professes faith in Christ; that's more than two billion people who say they believe the Bible. If only a fraction of the body of Christ, Protestant and Catholic alike, capture a vision for obedience to Christ's command to love our neighbors, a difference will be made. Not only that, but the wave of souls that are cascading off the cliffs of eternity will be turned around as the gospel is preached with words of truth and demonstrated with acts of kindness, compassion, and mercy. This is truly not a matter of good works, but a response of faith from those who have experienced the reality of grace.

The wave of souls that are cascading off the cliffs of eternity will be turned around as the gospel is preached with words of truth and demonstrated with acts of kindness, compassion, and mercy.

My experience with my old friends in Nicaragua reminded me just how impacting and essential the presence of authentic Christianity is to a broken world. The reason I was in Nicaragua was not to visit the city dump but to spend time encouraging, teaching, and equipping the national pastors and leaders of six churches this partnership had helped establish.

At that conference in the heart of Managua we saw it all happen. Through the financial support of Glenn's, Roy's, and Steve's churches in America, the Nicaraguan Christians were able to travel by boat or bus, some through the night, to get to the conference site. Many of them had never met each other, but the excitement of attending a conference for the first time put an electric expectation in the air from the beginning. For three days they built new friendships, ate meals together, sang songs of worship, received teaching, and ministered to one another hour after hour. They were hungry for information and fellowship in a way that I hadn't experienced for some time. This revived and renewed my love and passion for being part of God's intervention in healing and restoring a society through the establishment of healthy discipling churches that exemplify the gospel through both words and works.

The Gospel of Hope

There is a kind of power in the presentation of the gospel that is beyond all human reasoning. It is a message of hope and has an unexplainable, supernatural ability to instill hope. The gospel is a message of new beginnings and second chances. It is a message of healing, restoration, and renewal. The gospel message is fresh water for parched, dying soil. It is a living message that has to be experienced to be believed or fully understood. It is a message of God's desire to intervene and resuscitate the hopeless and dying human heart. The gospel alone holds an invisible and miraculous quality that can instill faith and bring substance and assurance to hope (see Heb. 11:1). When it is embraced and received, it cleanses destructive memories, heals lifelong emotional wounds, forgives actions that cause guilt and shame, and provides the grace to let go of rage and anger rooted in the memories of past offenses. The gospel, and only the gospel, can change everything. It can change entire societies by changing one heart at a time.

> *The gospel, and only the gospel, can change everything.*

Recently I was reading an article by longtime English news columnist Matthew Parris. Parris is a professed atheist with a heart that desires real change for the devastation of extreme poverty in Africa. After a recent visit to Malawi, he came to an amazing realization, which caused him to recount his experience in his column. He wrote,

> Now a confirmed atheist, I've become convinced of the enormous contribution that Christian evangelism makes in Africa sharply distinct from the work of secular NGOs, government projects and international aid efforts. These alone will not do. Education and training alone will not do. In Africa, Christianity changes people's hearts. It brings a spiritual transformation. The birth is real. The change is good. I used to avoid this truth by applauding—as you can—the practical work of mission churches in Africa. It's a pity, I would say, that salvation is part of the package, but Christians black and white, working in Africa, do heal the sick, do teach people to read and write, and only the severest kind of secularist could see a mission hospital or school and say the world would be better without it.[1]

Parris's words reaffirm what every true Christian instinctively knows—there is an unexplainable power in the gospel. Faith in Christ can change the world more effectively and more efficiently than any secular social work. Wherever spiritual deadness is present in the world, there is hopelessness; and where there is hopelessness, there is despair and the escalation of crises and devastation of every kind. Wherever there is a growing Christian faith, there is a flicker of light that drives out darkness, bringing reformation that stimulates authentic cultural change. This is the work of the Spirit and a genuine touch of God's amazing grace. Often when I share these thoughts, I hear

1. Matthew Parris, "As an Atheist, I Truly Believe Africa Needs God," Times Online, December 27, 2008, http://www.timesonline.co.uk/tol/comment/columnists/matthew_parris/article5400568.ece.

the warning that this is what some would call the "social gospel," and the fear is expressed that we may miss grace for good works. From my observation, no one can or will last working in the midst of real poverty or pain if they are not authentically motivated by a personal experience with grace.

If we are to be effective as harvesters, we must embrace the message of the harvest, which is the message of grace. Remember what Paul said: "For it is by grace you have been saved, through faith—and this not from yourselves, it is the gift of God—not by works, so that no one can boast. For we are God's workmanship, created in Christ Jesus to do good works, which God prepared in advance for us to do" (Eph. 2:8–10).

We are saved by grace through faith for good works, works that we have been created to do and which God even prepared in advance for us to do. The work we do must be rooted in the grace and unconditional love of God, which is acquired only by way of authentic faith. No one is going to stand in front of a charging herd of scared buffalo (or a society that is headed for certain destruction) unless they truly believe in eternity and have been personally impacted by God's love in Christ. All our efforts would be dead and ineffective without an authentic encounter with God's amazing grace and his empowering presence.

The concept of grace is so contrary to human nature that it is hard to understand or even accept. We may believe we are unworthy of receiving anything from God. On one hand, we may feel insignificant like a small pebble on an endless beach, believing that God probably doesn't care about us and surely sees no value in us. On the other hand, we may feel that God does know us all too well and sees only our shortcomings and points of guilt and shame. Grasping the truth that God loves us and desires relationship with us can seem far too amazing to believe. The very idea that he knows us and has prepared good works for us to do even before we were conceived (Eph. 2:10) can seem unfathomable.

Grace comes to us through faith—even the little faith we might have initially. When we first give our lives to Christ, our faith is more a matter of childlike hope than any deep faith driven by theological understanding. I love the story in the book of Mark where Jesus was about to heal a man's son. He asked the man if he had faith to believe. The man replied, "I do believe; help me overcome my unbelief!" (Mark 9:24). I know that feeling very well. For all of us, in the beginning, have faith like a tiny mustard seed. By God's grace, over time, it can grow into a huge tree. That is, of course, if it's planted and becomes established in the good soil of God's love.

There is no question that the harvest is ripe in today's world and even right here in America. It is a harvest full of those who are mentally unaware that there is an assurance of eternity, a future, and a hope beyond the downward spiral of society all around them. Even so, God has already put in their hearts an undeniable desire to know. They long for healing in their broken relationships, relief from their guilty consciences, deliverance from their addictions, and the discovery of God's true purpose for their lives. They desire relationship with the Creator, seeking it through nature, rituals, and other avenues and not realizing that God is right here, waiting with open arms to embrace them.

This harvest of broken humanity is silently searching for those who are committed to the authentic ministry of Jesus—even though they don't even realize it. They want what Jesus has to offer but don't know how to find it. They want to become a part of a community of people who are full of mercy and compassion for those who suffer, a people who care about the escalation of global human injustice and are willing to get involved and participate in the solution. They are looking for the authentic Christian church that actively lives out the kingdom of God in both words and deeds.

The privilege of participating in God's harvest is the ultimate fulfillment of every believer who by God's grace grows to maturity. The journey to Christian maturity is a long and hard one. But when all is said and done, it is the only one that truly satisfies. Speaking of this journey, Jesus warned, "Small is the gate and narrow the road that leads to life, and only a few find it" (Matt. 7:14).

Yet when this journey is traveled and the gate has been discovered, it becomes every true believer's passion to help lead others to it. There is no greater reward than to be a laborer in God's harvest field, though the task seems overwhelming and beyond all natural human ability. It is only as we recognize that the Lord has ripened the harvest and made it ready for the picking that we will patiently roll up our sleeves and get to work.

Epilogue

A year passed since that day Nancy drove the old ranch truck and trailer out into the field when I baled the first hay at Timber Butte. I was overwhelmed with joy after having gone through so much to finally harvest and bale our own crop. It had been a long journey, yet one that ended with great reward. My tears were tears of thanksgiving.

A year after that, I found myself sitting on our back porch in the late evening after having completed our second season of harvest. This harvest produced nearly twice the amount of hay as the first one. As I watched a full harvest moon pass behind a cumulous cloud, I pondered the words of King Solomon when he said, "I know that there is nothing better for men than to be happy and do good while they live. That everyone may eat and drink, and find satisfaction in all his toil—this is the gift of God" (Eccles. 3:12–13). We had spent the day putting up nearly ten tons of hay in the barn loft and shed in preparation for the winter months ahead. We finished just in time to take cover from a great downpour of summer rain, a rain that could have ruined the hay with mildew.

I looked up at the magnificence of the evening sky as I sat there recovering from a stressful and physically taxing day of work. I felt a deep sense of gratitude and my heart overflowed with thanksgiving. We had been harvesting for a week: cutting, raking, baling, stacking—all the while fighting equipment malfunctions, intense heat, and the threat of untimely thunderstorms. In the end, God's timing was perfect and we were done. As tired as I felt, I was grateful that the hay was both dry and stored away and that the challenge of the task was over for another year.

I am keenly aware that not everything in life goes exactly as planned, and that more often than not, mishaps can interrupt expectations and progress along the way. But I also know that no matter how things go, if we persevere through the fields of life, in the end there will always be cause for thanksgiving.

That evening I was able to take great pleasure in the fruits of my labor. As Solomon had said, "There is nothing better for men than to be happy"—and there is nothing better than experiencing the fruits of one's labor, knowing "this is the gift of God." If this is true in the case of a small forty-acre hayfield, how much truer is it when we participate in the reaping of God's global harvest field—a harvest that will be stored away not for a season but for eternity!

It is the destiny of the seed that falls in good soil to grow to maturity and reproduce an abundance of new life. And it is the destiny of every mature Christian believer to join with many laborers in a harvest of human souls that God has supernaturally prepared for a great ingathering. To be invited to participate in this field of harvest is a gift from God and the most rewarding and satisfying endeavor of our human journey.

Tri Robinson is the founding pastor of the Vineyard Boise Church and author of *Saving God's Green Earth* and *Small Footprint, Big Handprint*. Tri and his wife, Nancy, manage an eighty-acre farmstead at the base of Timber Butte, about an hour from Boise, Idaho.

Also by Shapevine

Organic Leadership
by Neil Cole

9780801013102 • 320 pp.

"Neil takes the person, the context, and God's Word, and mixes them in a powerful way for a life of leadership. Absent from this mix is the Western-driven spirit of 'how to use people to get your stuff done'! This is a book on how leaders do life, develop others, and flow in the kingdom of God." —**Bob Roberts Jr.**, senior pastor, Northwood Church; author, *Transformation* and *Glocalization*

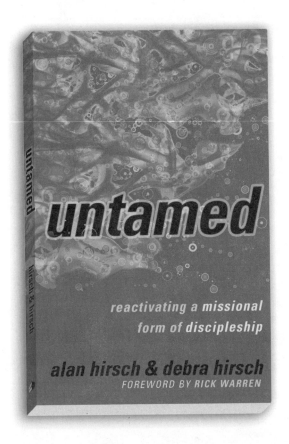

Untamed
by Alan & Debra Hirsch
9780801013430 • 272 pp.

"*Untamed* is a desperately needed shot of spiritual adrenaline into our mild-mannered and mediocre attempts at following Christ." —from the foreword by **Rick Warren**, author, *The Purpose-Driven Life*

BakerBooks
a division of Baker Publishing Group
www.BakerBooks.com